LOOSENING
YOUR GRIP

Letting Go and Living
in True Security

LOOSENING YOUR GRIP

Letting Go and Living
in True Security

HAROLD SHANK

— *A* —
FAITH FOCUS
Book

Sweet Publishing

Fort Worth, Texas

LOOSENING YOUR GRIP
Letting Go and Living in True Security

Copyright © 1995 by Harold Shank
Published by Sweet Publishing
3950 Fossil Creek Blvd., Suite 201
Fort Worth, TX 76137

Scripture quotations, unless otherwise noted, are from the Holy Bible: New International Version. © 1973, 1978, 1984 by the International Bible Society. Used by permission of Zondervan Bible Publishers. Those marked NRSV are from the New Revised Standard Version © 1989, Division of Christian Education of the National Council of the Churches of Christ in the United States of America. Used by permission. Those marked RSV are from the Revised Standard Version © 1952, 1971, Division of Christian Education of the National Council of the Churches of Christ. Those marked TEV are from Today's English Version © 1966, 1971, 1976, 1979, 1992.

Library of Congress Catalog Number 94-67235

ISBN: 0-8344-0237-8

Printed in the U. S. A.
10 9 8 7 6 5 4 3 2

To Sally:

אני לדודי ודודי לי

—Song of Solomon 6:3

Contents

INTRODUCTION

I'm Afraid of Falling

When I started to write this book I had two problems. One, I was trying to control life, and it wasn't working. I'd earned the equivalent of a Ph.D. in control. I'd read all the books on self-discipline. Management was my middle name. Despite my own iron will, I felt as out of control as a kindergartner on the first day of school. Despite my bookshelf full of how-to books, my life was a perfect example of "not this." Management may have been my middle name, but mostly I was Mr. Chaos. Gripping life was not working any more than holding on to the ladder helped my fear of falling. The tighter I gripped, the more I fell.

Two, since I couldn't control life, I wasn't sure what to do next. Nothing is worse for us control people than to see that our efforts at control are not working. Management techniques that work great at the office alienate my teenager, offend my wife, and have no effect on my two year old. The iron will confidence that makes me work through lunch, come in on Saturday, and make my secretary stay until 6:30 P.M. bends and cracks when I try to use it Sunday to make my heart praise God or Monday to convince myself that I'm managing my personal finances adequately. How can I breeze through the management seminar but fail to win the argument in the family car?

My problem with control is much like my fear of

heights. Climbing up my twenty-five-foot extension ladder to clean the second story gutters at the back of my house puts terror in my heart. I'll do anything to avoid climbing those fifteen fearful steps. Looking down from the top gives me that rare medical condition known as stomach-in-the-mouth. Occasions when the ladder shifts an inch or two, my whole life passes in front of me as I prepare to meet my death. The eighteen feet from my eyeballs to the flower bed mulch seems deeper than the Grand Canyon.

It's not just the gutters. The only way they could get me to walk across the Royal Gorge Bridge in Colorado was to let me straddle the two yellow lines in the middle of the roadway. I've never trusted a safety rail anytime in my life. I could never jump off Lover's Leap because I'm too chicken to get that close to the edge. At camp I always hated the top bunk. I'll look at your slides of Niagara Falls, but don't make me visit in person.

Actually, it's not the heights that frighten me. I know safety rails are anchored in concrete. I know some engineer has verified the safety of the Royal Gorge Bridge. My problem is that I'm afraid of falling.

The only way I can keep from falling is to hold on tight. Cleaning second story gutters is difficult work when you only have one free hand. My other hand is glued to the ladder. I try to overcome my fear of tumbling to the ground by tightening my grip.

My fear of falling goes beyond ladders and bridges. I'm afraid of falling in other areas of life. I'm afraid that if I don't hold on to my wallet, I'll fall into financial hard times. I'm afraid that if I don't control my schedule, I'll fall flat on my face in exhaustion. I'm afraid that if I don't keep a tight grip on my friends, I'll be alone. I even try to keep God close at my side in case I need his help. I tend to face all the heights of life in the same way: I tighten my grip. I try to control my life.

I've noticed an odd thing about cleaning gutters. The more I look down, the more frightened I become. The tighter my grip on the ladder, the tighter the fear grips my heart. Occasionally I get so involved in removing the leaves and acorns that I loosen my grip. There in midair, I realize I've also lost my fear. By concentrating on something besides my fear, my apprehension disappears.

I've found that true with the rest of my life. The more effort I make at regulating my time, money, and energy, the less time, money, and energy I seem to have. When I give control of my time, money, and energy to God, I end up more satisfied with all three. Every attempt I make to supervise how each week unfolds results in seven days of less control. Yet when I turn supervision of my life over to God, I find the pieces of my life falling together in the most unexpected and the most pleasing ways.

Control is my thing. All of us are into control to some degree. Each one has some irrational fear, like the terror of falling, that makes us hold on tighter. So in our own ways we try to control our schedules, our kids, our jobs. We keep a tight grip on our finances, our obligations, our future. Sometimes I find myself trying to control my wife. Sometimes I even try to control God.

To get to the heart of my problem, I began looking for the source. Let me tell you what I found:

- Life is often built around some big lies.

- I wasn't the only one struggling with control.

- Pretending can be bad.

- Surprises can be good.
- Poor people exemplify giving up control.
- No one is exempt from disappointment in life.
- Keeping score means I lose.
- House closings can become spiritual experiences.

You may be thinking, Does he really have control of his life now? Does he really know what to do next?

Let me just tell you this. My house has changed. I'm still afraid to clean the gutters, but I've learned about letting go. I know about the surprise that comes when you first release your grip. I know that I'm not the first one who tried to hang on for dear life. I know that letting go offers some lofty rewards. I know that releasing my grip is fundamentally a spiritual experience.

Best of all, I know that letting go leads to the greatest security I've ever known. Because it's been such a great journey for me, I just have to share it with you.

Luke 18:18-30

A certain ruler asked him, "Good teacher, what must I do to inherit eternal life?"

"Why do you call me good?" Jesus answered. "No one is good—except God alone. You know the commandments: 'Do not commit adultery, do not murder, do not steal, do not give false testimony, honor your father and mother.' "

"All these I have kept since I was a boy," he said.

When Jesus heard this, he said to him, "You still lack one thing. Sell everything you have and give to the poor, and you will have treasure in heaven. Then come, follow me."

When he heard this, he became very sad, because he was a man of great wealth. Jesus looked at him and said, "How hard it is for the rich to enter the kingdom of God! Indeed, it is easier for a camel to go through the eye of a needle than for a rich man to enter the kingdom of God."

Those who heard this asked, "Who then can be saved?"

Jesus replied, "What is impossible with men is possible with God."

Peter said to him, "We have left all we had to follow you!"

"I tell you the truth," Jesus said to them, "no one who has left home or wife or brothers or parents or children for the sake of the kingdom of God will fail to receive many times as much in this age and, in the age to come, eternal life."

Chapter 1

The Whopper

∽

There are lies, and then there are lies. I want to talk about the big one. Not the runner-up list, like:

- No, you didn't wake me up;
- *I* didn't leave the cap off the toothpaste;
- I *love* your new dress;
- I was just *kidding*;
- The check's in the mail.

The whopper I have in mind falls into a different category. It's not part of dishonest dialogue we have with others, but a lie we tell ourselves. It's not something we say to save face; it's something we believe that makes us lose face.

It takes me in all the time. Fish only get one chance, but I swallow this bait, hook, line, and sinker every day. I'm wise to most cock-and-bull stories, but not this one. Even when it's dressed up like a proper chicken and respectable cow, I fail to see through it.

Although firmly convinced of its falseness, I often build my life around it. This whopper runs my agenda,

7

guides my thinking, dictates my decisions. I vow never again to believe this sham, only to find it lurking in every act of faith. Every attempt to remind myself of this life-ripping prevarication falls to the floor like a worn out Post-it note.

Doesn't It All Depend on Me?

Maybe you have problems with the big lie, too? Maybe you've been taken in by this whopper.

It all depends on me.

The world will fall apart if I don't act. Masses of people will suffer if I do not respond. This family will fall flat on its face if I don't get moving.

The whopper tells me I'm indispensable. Nobody can do it besides me. I'm irreplaceable. Without my vital contribution, civilization as we know it would grind to a halt.

It all depends on me.

Five words that drive us to stay late, get up early, work with a headache, go in with the flu, and break promises. Five words that keep us from seeing the difference between being dependable and being indispensable, that blind us to the discrepancy between *irresponsible* and *irreplaceable*. It's a faulty belief that pushes us into overdrive when we should be in park, that destroys our spirit when we should be restoring our soul.

It all depends on me.

It seldom comes dressed that plainly. Typically it wears a costume that alters it almost beyond recognition. Not content to be merely misleading and untrue, it comes disguised as something else. I humbly follow it down the wrong road, thinking I'm on some sort of holy crusade. I end up thinking that I'm close to being the center of the universe because of the burdens placed on me. Because of its double dealing, I'm often dealt a double blow. Do you see it hidden behind these masks?

- *Disguise:* With pride we conclude nobody else is as qualified to do this as we are.
  Response: I'm the only one who can do it.
- *Disguise:* As we shake our heads, we sigh, "People don't care about these things like I do."
  Response: If anybody is going to care, it depends on me.
- *Disguise:* One of our excuses for working another Saturday: It's my job to do it, and if I fail I might be out on the street.
  Response: I'm indispensable.
- *Disguise:* Nothing goes right unless I'm there.
  Response: It all depends on me.

These little lines trick us into action, sometimes into energy-sapping activity. The whopper puts more cargo on our ship than we can bear. As we sink under the weight, we wonder who will take our indispensable place. We become martyrs for the cause until we sink into the muck on the ocean floor.

Believing the whopper makes me view all of life as something *I* do. Life becomes making a list and checking off each completed task. As I increasingly distrust others to accomplish their listed tasks, I become more convinced that I should trust only myself. I seldom rely on others because they have a history of doing too little, too late. I'm the only one who can do it. Life is a series of DO, DO, DO.

The whopper gets me all the time. It burrows into my thinking processes. Even as I write these words, a voice cries out deep in my soul, that says, *Are you being honest with these people? Don't you know that some things do depend on you?*

*Sometimes nobody else is as qualified as you.
What about the occasions where nobody cares like
you care? If you have the gift of efficiency, should you
not do the lion's share of the work? If you don't pull
your weight at work, you could be out of a job.*
*Don't mislead your readers. Some things do
depend on them. They are crucial in life's plan.*
(The whopper strikes again.)
Do some things depend on me? Is my interior
voice right? What about these things?
Nobody can love your mate except you. I need to
be a dependable source of love, but if she relies on
me for an inextinguishable source of affection, she
will be disappointed.
Your kids depend on you to be their parent. I must
be a reliable parent, but not an irreplaceable one.
Fatherless children often grow up quite healthy.
*Your job may hinge on your performance. You
don't want your family to be homeless, do you?* I
would argue, there are other jobs.
*Your salvation depends on a faithful life of Bible
study and prayer.* God provides salvation. The
spiritual disciplines are merely our maintenance
responsibility.
If you don't take the family to church, who will?
My inner voice may use guilt, as you can see. God
holds each person individually responsible.
*Jesus left it up to us to tell the world about God's
love. In a sense, the salvation of a world full of lost
souls depends on you.* That about sinks my ship.
Look at 1 Corinthians 3: I may do some planting and
watering. The increase is an other-worldly matter.
I hear these arguments all the time. That voice
whispers to me all day long, reinforcing the notion
that everything depends on me. If I don't do them,
they won't get done. If they are not done, the world

11

The Whopper

will end. Like a giant crane loading container after
container into my hold, the whopper keeps pushing
me deeper into the water.
You're indispensable. The ship settles another
foot into the water.
You're irreplaceable. Down another yard.
You're essential. Past the lower portholes.
We need you. Lower into the water.
We can't do it without you. A good wave would
now wash over the deck.
It all depends on you. My ship is sunk.
The internal commands pop out like bullets from
a machine gun. Make a list. Get it done. Do it now.
Stay late. Come early. Work through lunch. Don't
trust others. Work on the phone. Read on the bus.
The whopper wears me out. I'm not sure I can
survive life if it all depends on me. I'm not sure I can
cross a small river with that weight, let alone the
ocean of life. I'm just not made to carry that kind of
load. I need some help.
Even when I get one of those books about organiz-
ing my time, it only serves as a temporary fix. Read
the mail only once. Throw away unimportant things.
Don't delay making important decisions. Don't try to
do the work of other people. Divide stressful projects
into manageable portions, assigning each task to a
particular time. Prioritize things. Make lists. Reward
yourself when you get all the items crossed off.
It may help keep the ship afloat to rearrange the
baggage in the hold, but it doesn't alter the fact that
the whopper has overloaded my capacity. There's no
way that any list can hold all the things that have to
be done if it all depends on me.

Keeping a Checklist

I found another believer in the whopper in Luke 18.

There he was, another whopper-believing list maker intent on doing all he could. I thought I'd compare lists with the rich young ruler.

Luke 18:18-23 is actually a story within a story. We remember the main dialogue between Jesus and the rich young ruler. That's the inside story. As Jesus and the young man look at his list, another group stands to the side going over the same list. That's the outside story. We don't even hear from them until the inside story is over. But they've been listening all the time, and they are the real focus of the episode. I was surprised to find myself standing with that little crowd of people, mentally going over the young man's checklist as he spoke with Jesus.

Jesus began, "Number one. Have you ever cheated on your wife?"

The younger man shook his head. "No, I've been faithful." The disciples wordlessly echoed the same.

"Number two. Have you ever killed anybody?"

"No, I've never been involved in that sort of thing." The group silently concurred.

"Number three. Have you ever taken anything that wasn't yours?" I imagine the young man paused for reflection before affirming that he had never been guilty of stealing. The group experienced the same momentary reflection before drawing the same conclusion about their own lives.

"Number four. Have you ever falsely accused anybody?"

Surprisingly the young man didn't hesitate at all. "Never. From the time I was little, I've been totally honest in my relationships with people." The crowd did the same.

"Number five. Do you respect your parents?"

The young man gave his first affirmative answer. Not only had he not broken the negative rules, but he also kept the positive one. The silent crowd nodded in agreement.

"Number six. Will you sell your possessions, give the proceeds to the poor, and join the Christian crusade?" The victorious look on the young man's face faded into sadness. He had checked with his accountant and his real estate manager that morning. Investments were successful. Rents were all on time. The young man's silence betrayed his inability to let go of his bank accounts and land. That question hadn't been on his list. Jesus added it.

The young man was a list maker. He kept track of his moral progress. He was a *do*er. He thought it all depended on him. According to his list, he was five for five. Even five of six wasn't bad, but he could tell that it wasn't going to be good enough. Unable to answer number six with a yes and unwilling to make the changes so he could be six for six, the victory faded to sadness.

According to the earlier verses in Luke 18, the young man's problem surfaced long before the six questions. He approached Jesus with his checklist and a simple inquiry: "What must I do to inherit eternal life?" (Luke 18:18). Did you hear it? What must I *do*? He had the list in his back pocket. He knew the rules and thought he had kept them all.

I wonder how long the young ruler had been waiting to talk to Jesus. Had he listened to the two previous conversations? If he had paid attention to Jesus, he might have caught his own inconsistency.

Before meeting the young man, Jesus encountered some people who, according to Luke 18:9, "trusted in themselves" (NRSV). They believed the whopper. It all depends on me, they thought. I'm indispensable. I've got to be in control. Jesus exposed the whopper they had believed: "Everyone who exalts himself will be humbled, and he who humbles himself will be exalted" (Luke 18:14).

If you depend on yourself as you climb the ladder of life, you'll find that when you reach the top rung, you've come out in the basement of life. If you think you're producer, director, and leading lady all in one, you'll soon find yourself selling tickets. On the other hand, if you content yourself with selling tickets, you may find yourself facing a standing ovation. If you seek God's help in ladder climbing, don't be surprised at whose face you see when you reach the top.

What Must I Do?

In Luke 18:17, Jesus says, "I tell you the truth, anyone who will not receive the kingdom of God like a little child will never enter it."

Children major in dependence, not independence. Jesus found their simple, trusting nature a perfect qualification for admission into the kingdom.

How ironic that the self-sustaining young political figure was saying, "What must I do?" just after Jesus teaches that we need to be like children.

With his checklist in hand, he focused not on humility, not on dependence, but on items he may have omitted from the list. Concluding that his efforts had brought him close to the top of the ladder, he wanted to know which requirements he had to meet to vault himself over the top. Sure that he was the star of the show, he wanted some last-minute advice on how to sharpen his performance to please the critics. No longer a child, he wanted to show he was in complete control of life. "What must I do to inherit eternal life?"

Do you hear the inconsistency? He wants to *do* something to *inherit* something. Inheritance comes not by doing, but by being. My sons don't have to do anything to inherit my two old cars and collection of six over-the-counter stocks. They inherit because they are my sons.

The young politician felt so strongly that everything depended on him, that he would have _to do_ or _pay_ to _inherit_ eternal life. Since he believed everything depended on him, he thought that even the free things in life had a price tag. In essence, tell me how much I have to pay to get this free. Or, let me know how much work I have to do to get this gift.

People who believe in the whopper figure that there's a price on everything. Perhaps as the young man got dressed that morning he calculated, "I'll ask Jesus what I have to do to get eternal life. I think I've done everything necessary. If there's something missing, I'll do whatever it takes to get it."

He didn't count on being asked to quit depending on himself. His money was the rug under his feet. Jesus pulled it out. He was so used to buying what he wanted, he thought he could purchase a one-way ticket to heaven from Jesus.

That's the problem with those of us who believe the whopper. Once we believe we're indispensable, it's hard to give it up. Once we take the big step of believing that it all depends on us, it's easy to assume that everything at work revolves around our activity, and that family success falls on our shoulders. Then we make one additional step. What must I _do_ to inherit eternal life? Then we stand before Jesus with our checklist hoping we have enough to pay for the ticket to heaven.

All of that makes this a scary story. If the young man couldn't get out of the whopper's clutches, how can we? If the young man couldn't sell all he had, how can we? Those of us who believe that everything depends on us feel a strong need to explain this story away. We like to say, "This only applied to the young ruler because he was so tied up in his money. Jesus wasn't asking everybody to sell all their stuff." We want to be in control all the way through.

We maintain our control by looking for another way to understand the story. But we don't have to explain the story away. We just need to finish it.

Remember the silent list checkers in the outside story? Remember Peter and the other eavesdroppers? They were five for five with the young ruler.

Jesus said, "Number six. Will you sell your possessions, give the proceeds to the poor, and join the Christian crusade?"

The crowd that listened to the checklist process had great interest in the outcome. After the last question, the young man's head hung low, but the crowd held theirs high. After the young man left, still clutching his checklist, Peter was thinking that he came out pretty well. "I got six of six. I was with the young man on the first five. But unlike him, I got number six, too. I left my boat on the shore of Galilee. I left my profit-sharing plan. I left my house in downtown Capernaum. I left it all to follow him."

Jesus told the crowd that wealthy people would find it difficult to buy property in heaven. The words astounded the crowd. They had watched Jesus go through the checklist with the young man. They came to number six. Give up your money. The young man couldn't do it. Jesus affirmed that it would be almost impossible for a rich man to give up what was needed to get in. If a rich man couldn't give up enough, then how could anybody else give up enough?

What did that say for the listening crowd? Have we given up enough? What about the times we don't give up enough? How humble do you have to be? What if I have trouble being humble? Will I be on the outside of the kingdom? What if I have trouble acting as dependent as a small child? Will I find the gates of heaven locked? Who in this world can be saved if it's up to us to meet these tough entrance standards? If the people who couldn't give up their dependence on money couldn't get into heaven, then how could anybody get in?

It All Depends on God

Then come Jesus' magnificent words: "What is impossible with men is possible with God."

It doesn't all depend on me. It all depends on God.

Smash. With one line, he crushed the whopper. Not just the false belief that it all depends on me, but he also crushed its power over us. I find it as hard to give up the whopper as the young man did to give up his wealth. His money had the same power over him as the need for control has over me. He depended on wealth. I depend on myself.

Peter raises the practical question, "If we depend on you, will it work out?"

From where Peter stood and from where we sit, it appears that life depends on us. Peter's exact words are both boast and question: "We have left our homes and followed you." We've depended on you. Will it work out?

We know their puzzlement: If my job doesn't depend on me, but on God, will he keep me from being homeless? If I trust God with my family, will he see us through? If I give up my frantic attempt to be all things to all people, will I be anything to anybody? If I give up the whopper, will he support me the whole way?

Jesus knows about our insecurities. He knows the weight we carry. He knows how unsteady we are in the storm of life. Through Peter he reassures all of us who deny the whopper:

> There is no man who has left house or wife or brothers or parents or children, for the sake of the kingdom of God, who will not receive manifold more in this time, and in the age to come eternal life (Luke 18:29, 30, RSV).

What an insurance policy! Read the large print:

MANIFOLD MORE

IN THIS TIME

IN THE AGE TO COME ETERNAL LIFE

No wherewithalls. Not one "if the party of the first part." No exceptions for acts of God. From start to finish, it is an act of God!

MANIFOLD MORE smashes the whopper.

It all depends on me is tossed overboard in favor of *what is impossible with us is possible with God.* It lightens our load. It gives life integrity. It clears the way to see into the future.

It seems so clear. I know God is dependable. Nothing reminds me of that more than another crowd story.

Forty people elbowed their way to ask me questions. Everybody talked at once. We had just finished preaching to a capacity crowd at the Union Hall on the northwest side of Kiev, Ukraine. These people begged my translator to ask me certain questions. For nearly an hour we stood in the cold hallway going through the burdensome task of working between two languages (boy, I wished I knew Russian!).

Lyudmila was just a woman in the crowd. Not able to get my translator's attention to pose her question, she waited until the crowd dispersed. Then in her limited English she asked me if somebody would write to her. As I slipped her address in my coat pocket, I agreed to find her a pen pal.

Little did I know that she wasn't looking for a pen pal at all. She was looking for God. For most of our century, the Communists made him difficult to see. But she knew he existed. She wanted more than anything to see him.

Pressing her address into my pocket represented her trust in God. She had nowhere else to turn. She had no money. She had no well-placed relatives. Her job was not secure. Disabled by a serious illness, her husband was confined to his bed for most of the day. Three surgeries by local physicians limited by un-available medicines and aging equipment had made his situation worse, not better.

So she trusted God with that address—three lines that represented hope. She didn't come with a checklist boasting she was five for five. She didn't come saying "what must I do to inherit eternal life." She came, trusting that a man she had never met would somehow show her a God she desperately wanted to know.

Little did she know the difficulties God would overcome to see that she got "manifold more." My secretary, Marcella, wrote Lyudmila a letter, but it was delayed by seven Communist censors before it arrived at Lyudmila's mailbox.

On my next trip to Ukraine, I asked a Christian doctor to examine her husband, but the physician had the wrong speciality. Her husband had to suffer until we could return with a urologist. The doctors insisted that he be brought to Memphis for surgery, but the legal and financial barriers seemed insurmountable.

Then the doctors lined up to donate their services. A Memphis hospital waived all costs. Several Christians agreed to pay their airfare. On the day she and her husband applied for papers to the United States, they were two people among a thousand waiting in line. Yet that day the American embassy in Kiev issued two visas. Once on their way, all the problems seemed solved. Then a simple miscalculation about time zones led to one misconnection after another. This simple Ukrainian couple, who had never gone more than fifty miles from home, landed in New York City a day early. They transferred from Kennedy to LaGuardia by themselves, and arrived in Memphis at the very time that local Christians were at home coloring welcome banners. A security agent for Northwest Airlines provided their only greeting.

Two surgeries gave Lyudmila's husband a new body. Christ made him a new man. Now back home in Kiev, the woman who had trusted God with three lines of writing depends on her God just as faithfully now as she did then.

Impossible to depend on him? If you believe that, you'll believe any whopper.

It doesn't all depend on me.
It all depends on God.

Focusing Your Faith:

1. If you were part of Jesus' ministry team, how would you feel when the wealthy young ruler wanted to join your crusade? Why?

2. Jesus said the rich young ruler still lacked something. How would you explain what he lacked?

3. Money, possessions, and position were the rich man's "rug under his feet." What are yours?

4. How has the whopper, it all depends on me, invaded your decision-making?

5. What would it take for you to give God control over your responsibilities and concerns?

6. What have you given up as you follow Jesus? How has he replaced your sacrifice with "manifold more"?

7. Of the circumstances that worry you, which ones would you be willing to turn over to God to prove "what is impossible with men is possible with God"?

Luke 4:1-13

Jesus, full of the Holy Spirit, returned from the Jordan and was led by the Spirit in the desert, where for forty days he was tempted by the devil. He ate nothing during those days, and at the end of them he was hungry.

The devil said to him, "If you are the Son of God, tell this stone to become bread."

Jesus answered, "It is written: 'Man does not live on bread alone.'"

The devil led him up to a high place and showed him in an instant all the kingdoms of the world. And he said to him, "I will give you all their authority and splendor, for it has been given to me, and I can give it to anyone I want to. So if you worship me, it will all be yours."

Jesus answered, "It is written: 'Worship the Lord your God and serve him only.'"

The devil led him to Jerusalem and had him stand on the highest point of the temple. "If you are the Son of God," he said, "throw yourself down from here. For it is written:

'He will command his angels concerning you
*   to guard you carefully;*
they will lift you up in their hands,
*   so that you will not strike your foot against a stone.'"*

Jesus answered, "It says: 'Do not put the Lord your God to the test.'"

When the devil had finished all this tempting, he left him until an opportune time.

Chapter 2

The Do-It-
Yourself Life

❦

$\mathcal{I}$n their November 1987 issue, the editors of *Harper's* magazine wanted to sweeten the bitter juices of seven old "friends" of the human race—the seven deadly sins—by running a full-page ad for each of the sins.

What a spread. Let me describe this seven-page feature:

1. An obese man dives into a small pond underneath the caption: *"Be All You Can Be.* Sponsored by *The Glutton Society*, helping people make the most of themselves for over 100 years."

2. Santa Claus in a business suit sits atop this line: "The world's foremost authority speaks out on the subject of greed."

3. The third ad: "What luck! All the other agencies got the 'plum' deadly sins. Those lucky slobs get the sins you can really sink your teeth into. But what do we get stuck with? *Envy!"*

4. Wrath: "The only emotion powerful enough both to start a war [under the picture of Adolf Hitler] and stop one [under the photo of an antiwar

protest march]."

5. In the middle of a picture of the Garden of Eden: "If the original sin had been sloth, we'd still be in paradise."

6. The Pride Council of New York City sponsored the sixth advertisement. " 'Pride goeth before a fall'—we've all heard it. But how *TRUE* is it? It's mostly *BUNK*, agree today's top mental health experts. So stick out your chest, for heaven's sake. PRIDE—it's today's 'buzz word' for mental health."

7. Finally, "Any sin that's enabled us to survive centuries of war, death, pestilence and famine can't be called deadly." It's an ad for lust.

The tag team of *Harper's* and the best of the advertising world try to put a new edge on the old blades that attack all of us. They join a host of theologians and other practitioners who argue that these seven top the list when it comes to the biggest impediments in life.

Are they right? Are these the seven that drag you into the pits? What bothers you the most? Which sin disrupts your part of the human race?

Harper's didn't run the first article about sin. All three synoptic Gospels (Matthew 4, Mark 1, and Luke 4) report on the devil's attack on Jesus, the classic encounter of good and evil. Which of the seven deadly sins gets the most press in this debate? What weakness does the devil pursue in order to bring Jesus down? Which sin do we find buried in the contest between good and evil?

Satan vs. Jesus

For a long time, I thought that the temptation of Jesus had little to do with temptations that faced me. After all, I can't make biscuits out of rocks. I have no interest in politics. Climbing to high places scares me enough without even thinking of jumping. I was satisfied to believe that, although I felt no tug here, Jesus with his superior abilities found these temptations enticing. Is there something more to the threefold encounter?

It was an ambush. Scripture does not give us all the details. Did Satan jump out from behind a rock as Jesus sought a place to pray? As he sat by the campfire at night did Jesus hear evil noises beyond the light of his fire? Three times the wicked one invaded the private retreat of the Holy One. Led by the Spirit, Jesus was repeatedly attacked by the devil. Away from people, he encountered evil. Heaven and earth hung in the balance as the fight-to-the-death match unfolded. If Jesus sinned, the devil won. It was not best two of three, but sudden death. The bad guy could not lose. He would survive to fight another day.

The timing of the contest was incredible. Jesus left the Jordan River on a spiritual high. According to Luke's Gospel, the heavens opened twice in the first three chapters—two windows in the universe separated by thirty years. At his birth, the shepherds witnessed thousands, perhaps billions, of heavenly beings singing praises to God. The door slammed shut before they could catch their breath. The hole opened again after the baptism of Jesus. No billions this time, just a white bird and a man's voice. The Holy Spirit and the Father's speech. As the Spirit descended from overhead, Jesus listened:

"You are my son." God affirmed his ownership.

"You are my beloved son." God affirmed his affection.

"You are my beloved son; with you I am well pleased." God affirmed his approval.

Ownership. Affection. Approval. High accolades
from a heavenly source propelled Jesus on his journey. Luke then pauses to trace Jesus' family tree,
not just back to Mary and Joseph, but initially back
to the royal members of his genealogical background.
Not yet satisfied with royalty, Luke goes beyond
King David, showing Jesus' connection to the ances-
tors of the faith: Abraham, Isaac, and Jacob. Then
he drives the roots of Jesus to the deepest levels. He
runs the line back to God himself.

His approval rating high, his pedigree pure,
Jesus begins his ministry only to meet the devil face
to face. After forty days without even a snack, the
rocks started looking edible. The devil told Jesus to
turn the rocks into bread. Weak from hunger, Jesus
followed the stranger up the steep incline. At the
top, the two took in the panoramic view of world
political structures. Remembering that God sent
Jesus to start a kingdom, the devil offered him a
package deal: "All the kingdoms of the world if you
worship me." Moments later the devil brought Jesus
to the city where he would eventually die. He suggested that Jesus demand some protection, raising
the issue of whether God will rescue him from
threats on his life.

Which of the seven deadly sins does the devil use?

1. Gluttony? A bit of crust after forty days hardly
amounts to the temptation of overeating.

2. Greed? Jesus didn't want the wealth of earthly
kingdoms, just the open doors they would provide
into human hearts.

3. Envy? Jesus had little interest in the positions
the devil held.

4. Wrath? Injustice made Jesus angry. If the
devil took Jesus to a ghetto or leper colony, Satan
might have seen some righteous indignation, but

nothing about the bread, mountain, or temple top made Jesus hot. Those four don't seem to fit the three encounters between Jesus and the devil.
5. Sloth? Jesus spent the forty days in spiritual work. No temptation to laziness here.
6. Pride? The temptations show that Jesus did not let the Father's approval and the perfect pedigree go to his head.
7. Lust? The devil knew Jesus carefully directed his desires toward holy things.

The last three sins don't appear in the play-by-play. What temptation does the devil use? What's his angle? What lever does he use to pry Jesus away from his approving Father?

Self-sufficiency.

Temptation One: God hasn't given you any food, I see. Pretty hungry, aren't you? Better make up a quick batch of bread. If you depend on God, you might just die here among the rocks. Perhaps you should take matters into your own hands. You know you have the power to do it.

Temptation Two: God asked you to build a kingdom, I hear. Where are your advisors? Do you have an army? What kind of war chest do you have to finance this takeover? What connections do you have with the political machine? Did you study politics in Jerusalem? Since your Father didn't plan ahead on this matter, let me help you help yourself. I can arrange a deal on kingdoms. It won't cost you anything but your worship. This offer is only good today. If you don't do something soon, you won't have much chance of starting a kingdom.

Temptation Three: God promised to protect you. What if he's late? What if he hesitates? Is he really dependable? It's one thing to send the dove and speak from heaven, but will he be there to stop the penetrating knife in the crowd or the falling rock at the edge of one of these dangerous cliffs? Have you tested his reflexes to see if he'll be there when you need him? I sure wouldn't expose myself to the people who live around here without some prior testing of my security system. You better do it yourself to make sure he's going to be there.

The devil's words boil down to one thing: Be in control. Don't trust God to control your life. Control it yourself. It all depends on you.

Somehow we don't expect Jesus to face the same temptation we face. I have trouble giving control over to God. I have trouble with the big whopper. I want to run things. I want to hold on to that one piece of power that gives me some leverage in life. I want the certainty of looking over the plans prior to their release.

God the Son was tempted
to step in for God the Father.

This temptation lurks everywhere: When it absolutely, positively has to be there. Be all that you can be. Who could ask for anything more? Don't leave home without it. No wonder *Harper's* had to ask Madison Avenue to run ads on the seven deadly sins. They may be seven human weaknesses, but nothing sells like being in control.

What's incredible is that the devil knows it, too. "Jesus, you've got to be in control."

Jesus faced the same temptation!

God the Son was tempted to step in for God the Father. Jesus in the flesh enticed to play the role of the heavenly director. Not greed or gluttony. Not lust or laziness. Not anger, envy, or pride, but self-sufficiency.

I missed the point. How could I have read these verses, translated these sentences, preached this text, and missed the message? If there's anything that we control people don't want to hear, it's this point: Give up control. What could smash my need for control more than to realize that Jesus himself resisted taking control from the Father? What could stomp out my belief that it all depends on me better than to see Jesus rejecting that philosophy at the beginning of his ministry?

"Make your own food, Jesus."

"Build your own kingdom, Jesus."

"Make sure God's on call, Jesus."

Three times the devil got the same answer: "No. No. No."

Jesus saw the control issue. "People don't live by bread alone. I don't depend on myself for food; I depend on God.

"I don't depend on myself or on you for a kingdom. I worship only the Lord my God.

"Just because the Israelites put God to the test with their efforts to control their lives, don't think that I will do the same thing. It's not up to me to dictate to God how he will guide my life."

Jesus trusted God. He trusted God with his life. Forty days without food, but God will provide. He trusted God with his kingdom. Thirty years old and no following at all, but God will provide. He trusted God with his future. Three years until he died in Jerusalem, but Jesus knew God would prevail.

But several issues about this encounter between Jesus and Satan bother me. Why did Jesus even agree to this confrontation with the devil? Why did the Spirit lead him to the wilderness? Why not begin his preaching right away? Why fast in solitude before preaching to community? Why face the wilderness devil before the synagogue demons? Why sit on the hard rocks before healing the soft hands? Why wait when God had arranged all the elements of success? The dove. The voice. The lineage. Talk about advertising! Why run these full-page ads and then close the store? Why the publicity if the preaching has to wait a month and a half?

Think about what Jesus took on his wilderness journey. He left his knapsack beside the Jordan. He took no weapons. He carried no food. He had no torch. He had no sentry. No knife stuck out of his belt. No steel-toed shoes protected his feet. No suntan lotion shielded the hot sun. He went alone. Jesus gave up control.

*Without blade or bread, he attacked
with humanity's most potent weapon:
dependence on God.*

All the manmade forms of protection for life and limb were left behind. Jesus became vulnerable. Exposed. Seemingly defenseless. Yet he was not without the protection of God.

One morning Jesus looked up. No longer alone, he faced the devil himself. More dangerous than the penetrating rays of the sun, more perilous than any wild beast, more hazardous than any narrow path, more alarming than any cold night, Jesus faced the embodiment of all evil.

Yet despite his human vulnerability, he was not defenseless. He had protection even without all the mechanisms of control. Without blade or bread, he

attacked with humanity's most potent weapon:
dependence on God.

At each encounter, he countered with the
strength of his father. He confessed his allegiance to
God. He stood with heaven. He sided with inspired
revelation. He took refuge in divine guidance.

Satan vs. Me

All my life I thought that when it came to the
temptations, I could not follow Jesus because these
temptations were not my temptations. I can't eat
rocks. Politics have no appeal. I'm afraid of heights.

Last month I read this story about Jesus' temptations repeatedly. Under a deadline to produce a piece
about this encounter, I found myself empty. I was
hungry to find the meat of the text. I was struggling
with what it meant. The ticking of the clock threatened me. For several hours the most profitable thing
I did was to clean the lint off my computer screen. I
never realized how much lint there is on an empty
screen.

Why can't I see the point? Why can't I think of
something to say? How does this text relate to me?
How can these verses be meaningful to people I
know?

Nothing.

I read the text again. I looked at what others had
said. I read the text again. Every idea ended up
abusing the text or missing people. I went to the
corner and prayed, only to return to the blank screen
for another couple of hours. I said more prayers. I
found more lint.

Then I realized I'd been in control. I had been
strong arming the text so I loosened up. "Speak to
me, God." Suddenly, the fuller meaning of the text

appeared. The more I depended on myself, the more lint I found. The more I trusted in him, the more the words began to flow. So I am able to do exactly what Jesus did. First, give up control. Enter the desert of human defenselessness. Go to the wilderness of vulnerability. Second, depend on God. Count on heavenly help in every earthly situation. Look above for every direction below.

I've never found it easy to do. It was especially hard on a hot summer night in 1978. We had gone to Milwaukee to plant a church. In the middle of a cold Wisconsin winter, we planted a seedling that immediately took root and shot up toward heaven. For eighteen months, people who came to know God made their church home with our congregation. The growth was so rapid that we had to sublet the office space where the church had been meeting and sign an agreement to rent an empty church building. Then it got hot.

Word came that July day that the owners of the empty church building had sold the structure. Another church would move in. We were out.

A homeless church? A congregation wandering in the wilderness? A flock without a fold? We were too large for any rental space, too small to buy what we needed.

We had our defenses up. Angry with God for giving us growth and then cutting us down, we moped, cried, debated, prayed, sulked, and pouted.

Finally, one night, sitting on the front porch of our Milwaukee bungalow, we gave it all to God.

"It's your church, God. Do with it what you want. You want us to die, we'll plan the funeral. You want us to wander around like gypsies, we'll buy the wagons. You want to pull out the rug, we'll sit on the bare floor."

We gave up control.

Then a large piece of affordable property came into view. All logical reasoning suggested that an infant church like ours should not take on such adult responsibilities. That's for mature churches. We're poor. We're young. We're inexperienced. The most expensive thing I'd ever bought was a '71 Pontiac Ventura.

We prayed again and decided to trust God for direction. We depended on him.

Eighteen months later, we put the finishing touches on our four-thousand-square-foot building sitting next to a freeway exit on six acres of prime real estate. The congregation tripled in size.

Our temptation was to take control. Only when we gave it up did God work his wonders.

It's a lesson I have to keep learning. To depend on God when I'm hungry, when I'm struggling, when I'm threatened is hard to do.

It's not enough just to realize that we have a problem with control. It's not enough to recognize that "it all depends on me" isn't true. Jesus leads us through the thicket to the two-part process of dealing with this demon. (1) Give up control; (2) Depend on God. Go into the desert without our own defenses. Give up the tools by which we dictate our lives. Cast aside the efforts to force life into our own preconceived patterns. Then depend on God. Let him satisfy the pains that hunger for control. Let him guide us to our destiny. Let him hold us secure on the treacherous edges of life's precipice.

Practice Basic Fundamentals

Although control has social and psychological implications, it is primarily a spiritual struggle.

Satan ran at Jesus with the dagger of control. Be in charge! It's one thing to see that our need for control overrides family, friends, and office. It's quite another to see our attempts at control in a spiritual setting. Watching Jesus shows us four important elements in the process of giving up control and depending on God.

1. Allow God to set the agenda. You can do anything you set your mind to. Setting goals, concentrating on a task at hand, and guiding our ambitions in positive directions find roots in Christian thought, but when we narrow our focus to the point that God and his concerns find no place in our agenda, we have struck a bargain with the tempter.

2. Make every minute count. Wise use of time is a common Christian concern, but running ourselves ragged as if the whole world depended on us is no better than making biscuits out of rocks. Make sure you let God control your time.

3. Choose your fight. Christ called us to be ready to die for a cause. Just make sure it's not a selfish one. Make sure you fight under the Christian colors, not your own private banner.

4. Never give in. Persistence is a Christian virtue. Insistence is the product of a soul set on control. Repentance is nothing more than giving in to God. Commitment grows out of discipleship, but stubborness is simply a vehicle of control.

Like Jesus, our struggle with control is a spiritual war between the forces of good and the powers of evil.

Jesus' encounter with self-sufficiency also reminds us that giving up control once is never enough. Three times Satan pushed Jesus to the wall.

Take control, Jesus. **No!**

It all depends on you, Jesus. **No!**

Take matters into your own hands, Jesus. **Never!** Giving up control becomes part of the basic fundamentals of the Christian warrior. It becomes the daily dressing routine. Take up your cross (give up control) daily. Some of us controlaholics may find it necessary to turn things over prior to morning coffee break (or even before finishing the breakfast bran muffin). It's like mowing the grass or doing the laundry—it's never done. Never packed away and forgotten. In one wilderness trip, Jesus faced it three times. We will, too.

Jesus' experience with the devil suggests that our toughest encounters with self-sufficiency may come when we least expect them. Jesus was on a roll. "Not now. The voice. The pedigree. I'm in the spotlight, don't send me to the desert. Let me do what I came to do."

Nothing falls within our realm of power more than timing.

- "Let's make that 9:15 instead."

- "It has to be here tomorrow. No ifs, ands, or buts!"

- "I want the whole presentation to go exactly right. Make sure everybody is there on time. What we don't want is something like a late caterer or a slow parking attendant."

- "Look, I'm already late. You're just going to have to do it later."

- "Here I am, in the prime of my life, and I'm doing this!"

That's when the devil hit Jesus. He was in stride. He was on his way. Then the orange detour sign appeared on the road ahead: Forty-day Detour to the Desert.

Not now. Now.

Our struggle with control can't wait. You can put down this book, ignore the summons, pretend like you've conquered your self-sufficiency, assign it to your secretary, or promise to do it after the soccer game on Saturday, but it won't wait. If I am going to give up control, I have to give up control of time. If I think that I can schedule the hour when I give up control, I'm operating on self-sufficiency. Our encounter with control doesn't wait until we have a moment. Like the desert experience, it catches us midstride. It attacks us just as we leave the ground. It strikes just when we're up and running.

Until we willingly follow the Spirit into the lonely recesses of our soul, face up to the hunger in our stomach, struggle with who is in charge of the world, and turn our security over to him, we are still in the driver's seat calling the shots.

Ultimately it's not gluttony, greed, or envy. Likely most of us are not as deeply troubled by anger, sloth, pride, or lust as we are by one other more serious, more deadly sin. It's an eighth deadly sin that gets us in trouble with the first seven: We face the lifelong, daily task of giving up our self-sufficiency.

Until we willingly follow the Spirit into the lonely recesses of our soul, we are still in the driver's seat calling the shots.

Focusing Your Faith:

1. If you were commissioned to illustrate an ad for the "eighth" deadly sin, how would you depict control?

2. When have you "been on a roll," only for God to allow a confrontation with Satan's temptation?

3. If you were to meet the devil in the desert, what temptations of self-sufficiency would he use on you?

4. Name an example of how, even though you trust God to provide for you, you still have a plan B in case God doesn't come through the way you think he should.

5. Jesus fought Satan with humanity's most potent weapon: dependence on God. Why is that such a powerful force?

6. What situation in your life needs to come under God's total control? How might the outcome affect your ability to share your faith testimony with others?

7. Reread the Practice Basic Fundamentals section in this chapter. Which of these would be most beneficial to you today?

Luke 1:46-56

And Mary said:

"My soul glorifies the Lord
*   and my spirit rejoices in God my Savior,*
for he has been mindful
*   of the humble state of his servant.*
From now on all generations will call me blessed,
*   for the Mighty One has done great things for me—*
*   holy is his name.*
His mercy extends to those who fear him,
*   from generation to generation.*
He has performed mighty deeds with his arm;
*   he has scattered those who are proud in their*
*   inmost thoughts.*
He has brought down rulers from their thrones
*   but has lifted up the humble.*
He has filled the hungry with good things
*   but has sent the rich away empty.*
He has helped his servant Israel,
*   remembering to be merciful*
to Abraham and his descendants forever,
*   even as he said to our fathers."*

Mary stayed with Elizabeth for about three
months and then returned home.

Chapter 3

Surprise—God's Standard Procedure

∽

Walnut Grove Road bisects nearly the entire length of Memphis. Four miles of it belong to me. I don't own them of course, but it's the stretch I drive every day. Cutting through one of the most beautiful residential areas in our city, the street offers a pleasant, scenic drive.

But it's terribly routine. I know which tree turns first in the fall, and I can point out the section where the trees leaf first in the spring. I know the giant oak that stretches out over three lanes of traffic. I know which house has the Coors sign in the kitchen window, which houses are being remodeled, which ones are getting new shingles, and which ones are having driveways replaced.

Not only do I know the scenery of Walnut Grove Road, I know the people. Traffic in the morning moves quicker in the left lane. The going-home people tend to drive faster on the outside (except for the hill above the Perkins intersection where the right lane always slows). People always swerve to miss the potholes at Graham. That's also where people run the most red lights. The Goodlett intersection has the most accidents.

You get the message. I know the terrain. The opening chapters of Luke are like Walnut Grove. We go over that stretch every Christmas. We know the lines by heart:

"In those days Caesar Augustus issued a decree that a census should be taken . . .

"There were shepherds living out in the fields nearby, keeping watch over their flocks at night. . . .

"Suddenly a great company of the heavenly host appeared with the angel, praising God and saying, 'Glory to God in the highest' . . .

"But Mary treasured up all these things and pondered them in her heart."

Not much new here. Mostly well-worn paths. We've been down that road before.

Then I got to thinking about my daily trips down Walnut Grove. What kind of trees nearly hide the speckled pink house from view? Name the five intersecting streets between Graham and Goodlett. What kind of house sits across the street from the big mansion that always catches my eye? Is there a left turn arrow at Goodlett? What's the name of the academy just west of Mendenhall?

I . . . don't know.

How can I go down the same worn road twice, occasionally four times, a day, and not know the answers to such basic questions? I thought I knew that street. Maybe I should look again.

Routine Surprises

Look at Zechariah. Put yourself in his sandals the morning he left his quiet home in a Jerusalem subdivision. Zechariah and Elizabeth's place had

always been peaceful; they'd never had kids. Every
day brought the same routine. Elizabeth kept
Zechariah's house. Zechariah kept God's house.
Down the hill, across the valley, up the steep steps
to the temple. Animals to sacrifice, incense to burn,
sins to forgive. Routine stuff for the elderly priest.
He'd been down that road before.

Then one morning it was different. Maybe the fire
wouldn't start or the incense box was empty or the
table needed cleaning, but something made Zechariah look up. Not just look up, but he looked up and
right. Instead of just the carbon-stained wall he had
seen before, Zechariah saw an angel. Used to the
routine, expecting the expected, the unexpected sent
a chill down his spine and terror across his face.

Get up. Eat breakfast. Hurry to the temple.
Put on the ephod. Gather the kindling and the
incense. Check the crowd.

Light the incense. Say the prayer. See an angel.
Return to the people.

See an angel?

Hardly routine stuff, even in the broad experience
of a seasoned temple priest like Zechariah.

Yet the day of surprises for Zechariah was just
another workday for his heavenly counterpart,
Gabriel. Nobody knows the hours angels work, but
we do know something of their routine. God sends
them on a mission to a particular person. The individual is always shocked at the sight of an angel.
The standard response is for the angel to say, "Do
not be afraid."

Gabriel arrived on time in the temple that morn-
ing. At the correct moment, he appeared to
Zechariah just to the right of the incense table.
Gabriel saw the predictable look of terror on
Zechariah's face. Gabriel offered the reassuring, "Do

not be afraid." Once the angel got Zechariah settled down enough to hear his message, Gabriel told him to get ready for the patter of little feet.

More shocking than what happened in the temple that week was what happened in Elizabeth's womb. Not a routine time for Zechariah.

Turn the page in Luke 1. Mary was on a routine mission. Maybe she had gone to the spring to replenish the family water supply. Perhaps she intended to go to the market to buy some cucumbers or beans. Maybe she was out gathering firewood for the evening meal. Standard stuff for a young woman of her age.

As she walked along she probably thought of Joseph. She could smell the sawdust in his beard, see the rough callouses on his hands, and sense the reassuring nature of his affection for her. Whatever passed through her mind on this typical day, all of it jerked to a stop when she heard the angel's voice.

Zechariah was troubled by what he saw. Mary was bothered by what she heard.

"Greetings, you who are highly favored!"

"Favored?"

The eyes that were filled with love for Joseph now filled with terror. Favored by whom? Favored for what? Do I get any choice in this "favoring"? Since she was already the favorite of Joseph, she may have wondered about her being favored by somebody else.

Standard stuff for angels. Gabriel knew exactly what to say. Happens all the time.

"Do not be afraid, Mary."

What was a new experience for Mary was old hat for Gabriel. The road she freshly trod was one he'd been down many times before. He knew exactly what to say. He knew exactly how to explain the situation to Mary.

Zechariah couldn't believe that an old man like himself could have a child with an old woman like Elizabeth. Mary couldn't believe that a young woman like herself could have a child without a man. Gabriel managed to explain the unusual circumstances to both of them. Routine stuff for an angel.

We know most of that story. We've heard it since we were kids.

The God who picks a teenager in Galilee is full of all sorts of surprises.

Remember hearing this?

"God is going to pull the rug out from under the rich and put the poor in the choice spots. The God who picks a teenager in Galilee is full of all sorts of surprises. He'll feed the hungry who didn't expect to eat today. The rich will leave the dinner table hungry—surprised they didn't eat at all."

That's a rough translation of the song Mary sings. Missed it? Look at Luke 1:46-56. A song of surprises. Mary puts into poetry the words that her son Jesus will put into action. His life will be far from routine. He'll upset most of the status quo. Based on what's happened so far, we might call him God's biggest surprise.

Listen to another turn of events in Luke 1: Elizabeth calls for the midwives. Somebody starts to boil water. Another woman rips up an old sheet. Labored breathing. Elizabeth screams. Mumbled voices. Slap. And a baby boy lets out his first cry.

The first sounds from John the Baptist come out of the back room. The midwives wash up. They leave mother and baby a few minutes to get acquainted.

All the neighbor women gathered around the kitchen table waiting for the family to announce the name.

"They'll name him after Zechariah. He's wanted a son all his life."

"No doubt about it. Zechariah's the name."

They named him John.

"John? There's nobody in the whole family named that. Check with Zechariah. I bet he'll tell you the baby is to be called Zechariah."

The women hear the wax marker tapping on Zechariah's tablet. He hands it back. They pass it around the table.

J-O-H-N.

"Imagine that. That's a complete surprise. I wonder where they got that name. Elizabeth finally has a child, and at her age, and they pick a name that's never been in the family. Nothing surprises me anymore."

Some shepherds got the day shift. Others worked at night. Except for an occasional lion, most nights went as expected. They'll tell stories about the exceptional nights.

"It was a month past Pentecost when a lion came up from Jordan . . ."

"As the camels passed by on the King's Road, a viper from the desert . . ."

"It was the worst rain I can remember. The sheep scattered and it took . . ."

But most nights were routine. Except this one. Gabriel again?

The shepherds looked up from their flock to see an angel hovering just above them. Expecting anything except an angel, fear filled the eyes of each shepherd.

Routine stuff for angels. The angel knew exactly what to say, "Do not be afraid." But if the angel's appearance wasn't surprise enough, his announcement was. "Today in the town of David a savior has been born to you; he is Christ the Lord."

Having babies was a new thing for Mary. Birthing a child in a stable was not a family tradition. But neither Joseph or Mary expected shepherds to visit, reporting that they had seen an army in heaven shouting about the birth of this baby. It seemed like nobody was asleep that night. Angels, shepherds, heavenly host, Joseph, midwives, innkeeper, Mary. Not a routine night at all.

Luke's first two chapters ring with surprises:

Zechariah is startled at the incense altar.
Elizabeth feels the first signs of pregnancy.
Mary gets a surprise visit in Nazareth.
Mary says the unexpected after visiting her cousin.
There's the unexpected name.
Shepherds rub their eyes in disbelief.
There's the unexpected birth in the unexpected place.

Not a routine set of chapters at all. We're surprised. Gabriel wasn't. He summarized the message of Luke 1–2: "For with God nothing will be impossible."

No surprise is beyond our God. The unexpected is the routine with him. Surprise is God's standard procedure. It was. It still is.

Tears of Release

On Thanksgiving Day in 1993, about twenty of us from Memphis traveled to a small Ukrainian city called Bela Tserkva, which means "White Church." A dozen or so physicians and nurses spent the day with the local medical authorities while the rest of us taught about God in the public schools. With us were five Americans who planned to stay on in Bela Tserkva to minister the gospel. That last night together we preached about Christ in the city's main auditorium.

Afterwards, it hit us that most of us were leaving, but Brian, Alex, Barry, Margo, and Brady were staying behind. In a small room off the main auditorium, we gathered around those five. Each one of us put our hands on their shoulders. We wanted to pray to God for their safety and success by expressing our own solidarity before him. One of the physicians led us in prayer.

Then it happened. I just started crying. Big tears flowed down my cheeks. It startled me. I don't cry much. Tears don't come easily.

I'd often wondered why Jesus cried so easily. After his friend Lazarus died and sister Mary had issued the reprimand to him for not being there, Jesus cried. Why did he cry before he raised the dead?

Surely the words Jesus spoke as he overlooked Jerusalem in both Matthew 23:37-39 and 27:46 came out in phrases broken by sobs and tears.

"O Jerusalem, Jerusalem . . ."

"My God, my God, why have you forsaken me?"

At his own admission Gethsemane was a place of tears. The crying Savior pleaded with God as his closest friends slept. Both the impending events and his inattentive friends drove him to tears.

Did he cry on the cross? Was there a sob instead of a comma between "my God" and "my God"? Both blood and tears flowed at Calvary.

With my hands on the shoulders of Brian and Barry, my tears flowed freely. It was so sudden, so unforeseen, so unexpected. Later, I talked to several others in the group. I learned they had cried, too.

Months later I'm better able to understand my tears. For a year, I had prayed that God would open a door for us in Bela Tserkva. We had no money for missionaries. We had no expertise in cross-cultural missions. We had no people ready to go. Daily I made my request to God. Then in August came a letter from Brian, a call from Barry and Margo, and a visit from Alex. God had formed a team. Then one of our church's elders made a trip to Ukraine to find them teaching positions. The major university in town desperately wanted them to work on their staff, but they had no funds. The mayor of culture contacted another school on our behalf. They wanted all four to come. Housing was arranged. Letters of invitation were delivered. Then on the American Thanksgiving Day, we stood in Bela Tserkva asking God to watch over his workers in that city.

My tears reflected the overwhelming awareness that God had done what seemed impossible. Standing in the middle of what had been a godless Communist nation just twenty-eight months before, we witnessed God opening doors that had seemed forever nailed shut.

Zechariah saw. Elizabeth felt. Mary heard. Mary spoke. The parents named. The shepherds praised. And I cried. All because God had done something none of us expected.

Luke 1–2 also tells another story. As the story unfolds, Luke reveals the familiar struggle over control. Listen to the grappling for power as Zechariah reluctantly releases control:

The angel answered, "I am Gabriel. I stand in the presence of God, and I have been sent to speak to you and to tell you this good news. And now you will be silent and not able to speak until the day this happens, because you did not believe my words, which will come true at their proper time" (Luke 1:19, 20).

Zechariah wasn't willing to let go. He didn't believe, and now he couldn't speak.

The shepherds, also trying to stay in control, hesitantly agreed to investigate: "When the angels had left them and gone into heaven, the shepherds said to one another, 'Let's go to Bethlehem and see this thing that has happened, which the Lord has told us about'" (Luke 2:15).

Unlike Zechariah and the shepherds, Mary willingly complied: "I am the Lord's servant," Mary answered. "May it be to me as you have said" (Luke 1:38).

Quite unexpectedly, this familiar story outlines an important aspect of submitting ourselves to God. We can't predict his ways. We can't control his response. We can't anticipate his reaction. Even Gabriel, who had been down this road many times before, couldn't foresee all the details of what God would do next. All he could do was echo the centuries-old summary of God's work: "For nothing is impossible with God" (Luke 1:37).

WARNING!
Giving control to God
may turn your world upside down!

Ask Zechariah, ask Elizabeth, ask Mary, but don't ask Gabriel.

Forget Long-range Plans

I don't like surprises. If I liked surprises, I'd drive to work a different way every day. I like my routine of driving down Walnut Grove. That's why I want to be in control. If I'm driving the car, at least I'll know what to expect. Let me make the decisions so I'll

know what's around the next corner. Don't make me
live in a world where I'm not in control because I
suspect it's a world where my precious routine will
be spoiled by the unexpected.

God must delight in upsetting our long-range
plans. Things were quite exciting for one Memphis
church back in 1980-81. Based on a 1976 study to
provide room for growth, the church decided to add
two new wings to the church facility. It would only
be possible if the congregation could raise one million dollars in cash. Only a handful of churches of
any stripe had done that by 1979. They prayed. They
set the date. They encouraged each other. Families
talked about it around the dinner table. Finally on
April 27, 1980, they took up the long-awaited collection. The final tally was $1,025,000.00! Nickels from
children, stock portfolios, family jewelry, and even a
promise of an old pickup truck made the building
project a reality. God had blessed them with exactly
what they had planned.

Fifteen years later I paged through the small
print of their long-range plan. For years nobody had
studied the long-range agenda. They speculated that
by 1985, Sunday school attendance would be 1500,
with over 2000 in assembly. The 1985 reality was
661 in Sunday school and 1016 in assembly.

As I chewed on that disappointing news, I wondered where God had been for that decade and a
half. Then I began calculating. During that period,
there were a couple of domestic church plantings,
dozens of new congregations in Papua New Guinea,
establishment of a mothers' day out program, a
preschool, and a Christian elementary school, the
beginning of a para-missionary training program
aimed at putting one thousand workers in the field,
the launching of an inner-city job training program,

the successful work of a commodities closet for
people who use food stamps, a free child-care program for disabled children, a missionary team in
Argentina, a couple of churches started in Ukraine,
and the conversion of enough international students
at the local university to begin a church in their
homeland of Taiwan.

God had been busy.

None of it had been in the Long-range Planning
Report, dated August 20, 1976. None of it seemed
directly connected to the gifts of heirloom jewelry or
the Dodge Ram truck. Just as the isolated appear-
ances of an angel to an old priest, a young girl, and
the night-shift shepherds seemed to have no connection to a first-century observer, behind the scenes of
Gabriel's work and the Memphis ministry is a God
doing impossible things that we never expected.

Does that mean we should throw out our strategic
planning manuals and never talk to our children
about their career plans? Should we look to God to
deliver tomorrow's agenda in a plain, unwrapped
package in the mail? Not at all. But perhaps we
should do our long-range planning in pencil, not pen.
Maybe we should talk about the future with our
children with the full understanding that a key
player is moving backstage in ways we can't fathom
or know. Set up tomorrow's schedule, but make a
note in the back of our minds that somebody else
may need a last-minute appointment.

Be Open to Surprises

Giving up control means being open to the unexpected acts of God. Ask David and Joy Gibbs. Part of
submitting to God was becoming members of the
Impact church in the inner city of Houston. One
word describes this church: unexpected. They meet

in a warehouse, not a church building. They have two Sunday morning services, one in Spanish at the warehouse, another in English at a rented gymnasium two miles away. Expect the unexpected person to sit down next to you. It could be a wealthy couple from a distant suburb or a homeless woman from a nearby underpass. It might be two Christian college students doing an internship or a crack mother who's been straight for three months. David and Joy expected the unexpected.

One day people from Impact met Selia on a park bench outside the rented gym. The litter-strewn park reflected the inner chaos of her life. The Impact family adopted her. She learned that Jesus would remove her sins, but not her AIDS. As the disease progressed, so did Selia. One day she told the church that she had three final wishes. (1) Before she died she wanted to see her daughter Symntha baptized into Christ; (2) she wanted one more Christmas with her three children; (3) she wanted her three children to be adopted by a Christian family.

She watched one Sunday morning as Symntha was baptized.

Selia died a month after Christmas.

David and Joy Gibbs adopted her three children.

Zechariah, Elizabeth, Mary, and the shepherds would have understood. They knew about this God. He brings babies to the most unexpected people. Elizabeth and Zechariah, Mary and Joseph, David and Joy.

Ruth Harnden tells a story in her book, *Let Nothing You Dismay*, about an absent-minded older woman who mistakenly sent the wrong gifts out at Christmastime. She purchased a heavy pair of wool socks for a poor friend named Hilda, whose substandard house was always cold. She picked out a fancy lace nightgown for her attractive granddaughter.

By mistake, the granddaughter got the socks; Hilda received the nightie. The giver was horrified. She thought her granddaughter would think she was old and senile. She feared that Hilda would think that she was mocking her plain ways with the satin gown. After Christmas the older woman received two letters in the mail.

Her granddaughter exploded with gratitude about the fashionable ski socks Grandma sent.

Hilda's letter was ecstatic. Nobody had ever given her such a beautiful gift. "I put it on every night and dance across the rough, wooden floor, and for the first time in my life, I feel pretty."

That sounds exactly like something God would do. God does the impossible with the most unexpected people in the most unusual ways at the most surprising times.

> *The unexpected is the routine with him.*
> *Surprise is God's standard procedure.*

Focusing Your Faith:

1. If God surprised you with an amazing experience, how would you most likely tell about it: sing a song, paint a picture, write a novel, or make a video?

2. Do you believe that God still uses angels as messengers to humans today (Hebrews 1:14)?

3. In Mary's song, she praises God by singing his attributes. Read Luke 1:46-56 and identify the most outstanding attribute she names.

4. If you were one of the night shift shepherds, how would you have tried to explain away the angel's appearance?

5. If God were to answer your prayers in an unexpected way, would you respond hesitantly like Zechariah or willingly like Mary?

6. Recall something God has brought about that wasn't in your church leadership's long-range plan.

7. What in your life experience keeps you from expecting God's surprises? How could you begin to change your expectations?

Matthew 6:25-34

Therefore I tell you, do not worry about your life, what you will eat or drink; or about your body, what you will wear. Is not life more important than food, and the body more important than clothes? Look at the birds of the air; they do not sow or reap or store away in barns, and yet your heavenly Father feeds them. Are you not much more valuable than they? Who of you by worrying can add a single hour to his life?

And why do you worry about clothes? See how the lilies of the field grow. They do not labor or spin. Yet I tell you that not even Solomon in all his splendor was dressed like one of these. If that is how God clothes the grass of the field, which is here today and tomorrow is thrown into the fire, will he not much more clothe you, O you of little faith? So do not worry, saying, "What shall we eat?" or "What shall we drink?" or "What shall we wear?" For the pagans run after all these things, and your heavenly Father knows that you need them. But seek first his kingdom and his righteousness, and all these things will be given to you as well. Therefore do not worry about tomorrow, for tomorrow will worry about itself. Each day has enough trouble of its own.

Chapter 4

Don't Worry
about the Score

⌒⌒

$\mathcal{J}$ames A. Harding and Leonard Daugherty
teamed up in the 1880s to help churches. Harding
preached and Daugherty led singing. They charged
no fee for their services, but went to any church that
called. One January, the duo spent $37.10 for travel
expenses and advertising. The churches they served
paid them $1.50. They were short $35.60. Near the
end of the month they spent the night with some
Christian friends who handed them $13 the next
morning. A few days later Harding received a $25
check in the mail. Another man sent them $10. That
gave them a positive cash flow of $12.40, allowing
each man $6.20 to support himself and his family.

Their mission was an act of faith. They reasoned
that, if God wanted their work to succeed, he would
support it. If they put the kingdom first, God would
supply all their needs. Harding put it this way:

> If I had needed more money I would have re-
> ceived it. It is not necessary for a man to carry
> money about in his pockets that he has no need

for; the Father furnishes it as it is needed.

Harding went on to say that it wasn't always easy to trust God for the money.

It is hard to wait undoubtingly when you are hundreds of miles from home, without a dollar, preaching in a little log school house back in the woods among a half dozen or so of brethren every one of whom is poor, and every one of whom probably thinks that you, being a Kentuckian from the "Blue Grass," are rich . . .[1]

Harding let God control his future. Once, as he closed a preaching session some distance from home, his wife wrote saying that her money was nearly gone. Harding had no cash to send her. As he entered the railroad station for the train home, he received an envelope containing funds for the ticket. Later he learned that at the same time, his wife received the necessary support to continue the family life.

He argued that no Christian should accumulate more than daily needs. To spend Monday putting something aside for Tuesday showed a lack of trust in God. Use the money now for the kingdom.

That's pretty tough language. It's always bothered me. Does Scripture support Harding's view? I feel more like Joe Materialism than James Harding. Is there any place to stand between Peter, James, and John who left their fishing tackle in the Galilean sand to follow Jesus and the egocentric Herod who spent all the tax money on himself? Do we have to live like people in the first century or even in rural eighteenth-century America to seek first the kingdom of God? When we compare our lives to Peter, James Harding, or Mother Theresa, why do we feel we've lost the game before we've even walked on the court? Is there another way to play this game?

Keeping Score

You couldn't find a place to park. You could smell the popcorn. You could touch the tension. Saturday morning at one of the local high school gyms is the last place that I thought I would be on a crisp fall morning, the last place I expected to find a large boisterous crowd, and the very last place I expected to lose my cool.

First-grade basketball lacked nothing. Concessions. Cheerleaders. Coaches. Uniforms. Buzzers. Referees. And about one father-piloted camcorder for every two children on the floor. I brought my trusty 35mm camera with attachable flash (no camcorder at our house yet).

Four teams playing at once. Whistles from two games. Parents of the four teams on the floor sat as the parents of the four teams about to play waited in the wings. Congestion. Chaos. Confusion.

The accumulated debris from those Saturday mornings remain fixed in my mind:

- The father who criticized his child to tears before the parents of both teams;
- The angry coach who refused to abide by the parity rules and played only the best players;
- The mother who verbally battered the teenage referee each time the teams ran to our end of the court;
- The parents who acted like these gladiatorial games surpassed everything else in importance;
- The players who ignored the clumsy boy;
- The father surprised by his angry shouts and

feelings of hostility.

Few things in my adult life have caught me more off guard than my aggressive reactions to watching my children in sports. Why was I so angry at a coach I didn't even know? Why did I despise the first-grade forward who just happened to be tall for his age?

These Saturday morning fights all revolved around one thing. One issue made the coach angry, the father bitter, the team greedy, and the parents hostile. One thing raised the tension level in the gymnasium. One thing pitted first-grade boy against first-grade girl. One thing made the father bring tears to the eyes of his six year old. One thing stood behind it all.

We kept score.

We kept score because we wanted to win. Winning justified criticism, anger, battering, and insensitivity. Winning meant we had to be in control.

"Come on, John. You've got to do it. Fifteen seconds, John. John, move the ball!"

"Don't you remember what I told you this week? Don't you care about this game? Come on Billy, you can do better."

"Hustle, Jack. You look like a little old lady out there. Move it. We don't have all day!"

When we keep score, we have to be in control. Sometimes we keep score as we read the Bible. I did.

Matching Pieces

I listened with my imagination as Jesus worked his way through the beatitudes and the series beginning "you have heard it was said to the people long ago." People sat scattered across the Palestinian hillside. My family shared a large, gray rock with a Galilean family of four. I listened with two sets of ears. At times I heard his words in the context of the foursome at the other end of the rock. Sometimes I listened with my foursome in mind. As usual, I kept score.

As he put together the pieces of the kingdom puzzle, I compared myself to the folks on our left. They're from the first century. We're from the twentieth. Their footwear came from the shop down the street from their house. Our shoes were manufactured in southeast Mexico. They cook over an open fire. We eat supper out of the microwave. Their donkey gets fifteen kilometers to the bushel. Our Sable gets twenty-two miles to a gallon. (Score one for us; our life seems easier.)

Jesus' message moved meaningfully in both cultures until he came to the discussion about economics. Until then, he had carefully put together the puzzle pieces that we shared with the folks at the other end of the rock. But in the economic realm, I felt that Jesus mixed the pieces of two different puzzles together. His message fit them, but not us. Jesus picked up a piece of the puzzle that slid into a perfect nook in their lives. The same piece didn't fit our picture anywhere. He had to force his economic pieces into our slots. Nothing snapped into place as if it belonged.

Do not store up for yourselves treasures on earth (Matthew 6:19).

It fit the nice Galilean family. They had few treasures to store up—just the imported pottery vase from Crete and a gold necklace handed down in their family for five generations. Most of what they own they could carry on their backs. Most of what they own will be used this week to meet the demands of life. Such limited treasures didn't provide much to "store up."

To carry our treasures would break my back. Much of what I have is committed to my future well being. I have a hard time deciding what this piece of the kingdom picture means in my life. If Jesus means not to save any money, not to buy any insurance, not to plan ahead, not to invest in stocks, I'm guilty on all accounts. I've got quite a bit invested in what could be called "treasures on earth." (Score one for the Galilean family.)

Compare our family with that Galilean household. The dad probably worked with his hands. He taught his son a trade. The boy probably took over the family craft. I don't work with my hands. I have no craft that I can teach my children. If they want to take up my chosen occupation, they will have to go to college. His kids could pick from a hundred or so professions. My children could end up working in any one of thousands of different jobs.

Yet, I suspect I'm just as interested in preparing my children for the future as the Galilean dad is in preparing his. He'll take time each day to teach his son's hands to do what they need to do. I'll invest for college education. He'll let his son practice on a piece of wood that might have made a good chair. We'll put aside some money to take a family trip to visit two or three prospective colleges. In our own way, we each both prepare our children for the future. However, my preparations strongly resemble "treasures on earth." So when Jesus tells the Galilean father and me not to store up treasures on earth, the piece seems to fit his life better than mine.

Look at the birds of the air; they do not sow or reap or store away in barns, and yet your heavenly Father feeds them. Are you not more valuable than they (Matthew 6:26)?

The Galilean couple nodded with approval. Her

garden in the backyard filled the supper table. The
olive trees bore well. The chickens laid good eggs.
The old cow supplied the family with all their milk.
Whether birds or people, God provided.

At our house we have no animals or fruit trees.
The carrots we grew in the backyard looked de-
formed, the radishes were so hot we couldn't eat
them, and we raised a whole new generation of
tomato insects on the vines next to the air condi-
tioner. Milk comes from Kroger. Fruit from Market
Basket. Bread from the bakery on the south side.

No doubt, that Galilean mother cared as much
about feeding her family as my wife Sally does. Her
husband traded two chairs to Jacob down the street
in return for the iron kettle she used over the fire in
the courtyard, just as the fruit of my work pays the
grocery bill. They live close to the soil, in touch with
nature; we do not. Do we have to live on the land
and work with our hands to be eligible for the kingdom? Is there a contemporary edition of the kingdom
puzzle? (Score another lay-up for the Galileans.)

*If that is how God clothes the grass of the field . . .
will he not much more clothe you* (Matthew 6:30)?

If we actually stood alongside that Galilean
family, nothing would separate us more than the
way we groomed and dressed ourselves. Blue jeans
versus flowing robes. Shaven faces up against rough
stubble. Stretch socks or panty hose under Rockports
(Nikes for the kids) as opposed to bare feet in dusty
sandals.

Our lives call for a more complicated wardrobe
than the Galilean family could imagine. A coarsely
knit robe made of the wool from the family sheep
isn't an option for us in Memphis. Sandals leave
quite a different impression today. Jesus' image of a
simple body covering offers a piece that doesn't

easily fit into the modern picture.

Does God's idea of a wardrobe stop with the shirt on my back? How many neckties come with the "grass of the field"? Even if Solomon didn't dress any better than wild grass, most of us expect at least a little more variety. The promise of Jesus seems appropriate, given Galilean fashion standards, but so limited, so austere, so narrow when placed alongside the most recent Spiegel catalog. (The Galileans pull ahead on the score.)

Then we read the hardest text:

But seek first his kingdom and his righteousness, and all these things will be given to you as well (Matthew 6:33).

I suspect the Galilean family felt as challenged by this statement as I do. When all you own could be balanced on the back of a donkey, when all your liquid assets will fit in a tiny leather pouch buried in the folds of your only robe, when daily life consists of getting enough food, clothing, and shelter to make it through the weekend, the challenge to lay it all at the feet of Jesus must have chilled this man and woman to the core. Yet to risk it in return for a regular supply of clothes and food, to dedicate the two family donkeys, the cow, the fifteen chickens along with the vineyard and dozen olive trees in the backyard in turn for God's guarantee of survival may have enticed them.

It scares me. What does this text mean for a person who pays $1,657 each year in property tax, who owes a mortgage company in New Jersey 20 percent of his income to pay for a house in Memphis that is insured by a firm in Springfield, Illinois, that wants another $50 a month to protect that investment from fire and earthquake? Somehow I'm not sure that when Jesus promises that "all these things will be given to you as well" that he includes the mortgage bill, the car payment, and the balance on the Discover card.

I don't want to minimize the challenge that Jesus makes to my Galilean counterpart. Don't think that I necessarily want to trade my complex life for his simple one. Yet, as I keep score in reading through this text, the Galilean seems to win. He has less to give up. His kids are likely to be satisfied with less than my children. His food grew fifty feet away out in the backyard. My food grows five hundred miles away somewhere in the Upper Midwest. Am I wrong to keep score?

Quite frankly, if I give up control of my finances, my time, my food, and my shelter to God, it seems that I'm going to come out on the short end. Maybe it worked for Peter, James, and John, but it seems risky to me. The Palestinian peasant might come out a winner, but it looks like I'd lose the game.

The Perfect Scorekeeper

There's one other person keeping score in this Matthew text. Did you see it? Look at the scoring within the text. Notice the words I've put in bold:

Where your treasure is, there your heart will be also (Matthew 6:21);

Are you not **more** valuable than they? (Matthew 6:26);

Will he not **much more** clothe you? (Matthew 6:30);

Your heavenly Father knows that you need them **all** (Matthew 6:32);

**All** these things **will** be given to you as well (Matthew 6:33).

The other person keeping score in this text is God. Every time I tallied one for the Galilean family,

he tallied a couple for me. Notice the bold words:
more, much more, all, all.

If those scores don't convince you, try these:

*I have come that they may have life, and have it to
the **full*** (John 10:10).

*No one who has left home or wife or brothers or
parents or children for the sake of the kingdom of
God will fail to receive **many times as much** in this
age and, in the age to come, eternal life* (Luke 18:29,
30).

*We know that in **all things** God works for the
good of those who love him, who have been called
according to his purpose* (Romans 8:28).

*Do not be anxious about anything, but in every-
thing, by prayer and petition with thanksgiving,
present your requests to God. And the peace of God,
which **transcends all understanding**, will guard
your hearts and your minds in Christ Jesus*
(Philippians 4:6, 7).

Watch God do a slam dunk:

*Give, and it will be given to you. A good measure,
pressed down, shaken together and running over,
will be poured into your lap* (Luke 6:38).

God keeps score! His team wins! Every time! Not
only does the family with the donkey end up on top,
the foursome with the Sable wins! In addition to
giving us tomorrow's scores today, this text ends up
telling us three important things about giving up
control.

Playing Tips

1. Enjoy the Game

No text has puzzled me more than Matthew 6.
For a while I avoided preaching from it. I couldn't
find any sound economical advice to pass on.

Finally, I realized why this text was so difficult. I understood why it had become so hard to manage. In my effort to unravel this text, my main concern was to maintain control. The more I try to maintain control over this text, the more unmanageable it becomes. I want to control how much control I give up. I want to be in charge of letting God be in charge. I want to dictate how God dictates how I should live. My questions revealed my interest in control:

- Can I live in a nice house and have two cars?
- Is it okay to buy insurance?
- Should I feel guilty about having nice things when others don't?
- Does discipleship mean selling everything I have?
- Is James Harding right? Is it wrong to have a savings account?

Jesus has another list of questions:

- Can I live in your house?
- Where is your treasure?
- Do you understand that you are more valuable to me than any plant or animal?
- Do you trust me?
- Do you seek my kingdom first?

Jesus wants to know "Who is in control?" For Jesus, the issue is never economics; it's always lordship. Once I understand that the final score is already in my favor, I'm left free to enjoy the good things he gives me.

If I'm seeking the kingdom first, if I've given God control of my life, I can enjoy what he gives me.

- Do you have a nice house? Enjoy it. It's a gift of

God. Read Ecclesiastes 5:19: "Moreover, when
God gives any man wealth and possessions, and
enables him to enjoy them, to accept his lot and
be happy in his work—this is a gift of God."

- Should you put away money for the children's
  college education? Yes! God gives in manifold
  ways.
- Did God give you a magnificent car, stylish
  clothes, a great vacation? Yes! God has slam-
  dunked your life with blessings.

Who do you think made Abraham one of the
richest men in Palestine? Why should we feel guilty
when God presses it down, shakes it together, runs
it over the sides, and puts it right in our laps? That's
exactly what he said he would do!

The issue is not, Is what I have too much? The
issue is, Will I choose to put my life under the control of God? The first question can't be answered
until the second one finds a solution. Jesus himself
spells out the order: First, seek the kingdom. Second,
all these things will be yours.

Not everybody who has nice things has given
control to God. But if you've given control to God,
don't second-guess the rewards he sends your way.

2. Let God Change Your Goals

We all keep score. That's our problem with seeking first the kingdom. But once we know we're on
the winning team, keeping score becomes less important. In fact, kingdom seekers are amazed at how
their attitude toward the score changes.

When we seek the kingdom first, what we *want*
begins to change. Let me tell you about some of the
kingdom people I know.

Frank was on his way to the top. He understood
computers in a computer-driven world. Promotions

came as fast as new versions of WordPerfect. His climb to the top was as clear as the performance charts he turned out on the Laser Jet IIID printer. Then this young executive became a kingdom seeker. Suddenly the corporate world became less challenging than training and sending out one thousand missionaries. The corporate world became the means by which he would accomplish kingdom goals. Finally, he quit the corporate world to do independent consulting work so he could devote more time and funds to the work of missionary training.

When he gave up control to God, the things that caught Frank's interest changed radically. The number of missionaries in Malaysia is now more important to him than the number of terminals in the mailing department.

Another kingdom seeker's ministry is one of encouragement. Nothing delights my physician friend, Ed, more than handing the keys of his beach house to other families. He enjoys it so much, that about fifty times a year, he gives somebody the keys to enjoy the pure, white Alabama sand. It may be to a young couple for their honeymoon. Or, if somebody in church is going through a hard time, he might get a set of keys in his mailbox. When a family can't afford a vacation, Ed delivers the keys.

His generosity reflects God's control of his life. As he and his family make decisions about the use of the beach house, they pray that God will allow them to serve others with this gift.

Another kingdom friend, John, decided that giving up his job at the counseling clinic seemed the wrong economic thing to do. Going to Ukraine for three months to help encourage young Christians seemed the right spiritual thing to do. He gave two weeks' notice. He made the trip. God used the change

in his life to allow him to go back to school for a
needed degree.

Are you tired of keeping score? Sick of getting
upset when the nail-biter goes the wrong way? Fed
up with feeling guilty because you're not a James
Harding? Tired of wondering how you're going to get
all the ends of your earthly treasure to meet?

Good. The game's over. You've already won.

3. Don't Worry about the Score, Just Play the Game

Back to Saturday mornings: Do you know why
the dad criticized his first grader to tears? Do you
know why the coach played only the best players? Do
you know why I got mad at the tall seven year old?
We wanted to win.

But God says we've already won, and that
changes the game. It means we don't need to worry
about being in control.

That tall first grader wouldn't have bothered me
if I knew my child's team would win. Do you think
the coach would mind playing the less talented
players if he knew he'd be on top at the final buzzer?
Can you imagine any father upset enough for a
public tirade if he knew his kid's team had it in the
bag? That Saturday we wanted to be in control
because we thought that's what it took to win.

Take a look at my friends Sarah and Andy who
wanted it all. They wanted a van. The next Sunday
they arrived at church in their twelve-seater with
TV and VCR. They wanted new carpeting in the
family room. Workers quickly installed static-free,
no-track plush. He wanted a snowplow for his
pickup. Soon a yellow motor housing jutted out from
the front grille of his Silverado ready for the next
winter snowstorm.

There was one other thing Sarah and Andy wanted even more than the van. It was higher on the agenda than the carpet and more crucial than the snowplow. They wanted peace. The more treasures they collected, the more they wanted what they couldn't get. Despite their accumulations, life was chaotic. Together Sarah and Andy ran up a $35,000 debt on their credit cards. Money offered them no control at all. Putting plastic in their hands and checkbooks in their pockets gave them power, but no control. As their debt mounted their financial instability threatened their spiritual foundations.

God says we've already won, and that changes the game. It means we don't need to worry about being in control.

Sarah and Andy lived down the street from another Christian couple. Although both couples attended the same church, they claimed different relationships with God. Their neighbors sought God's kingdom by giving him daily control of their lives. They sold their house and moved to another to enhance their ministry. They prayed for the people in his factory to come to Christ. Sarah and Andy saw that these neighbors had what they couldn't get.

Someone suggested a radical solution. Sarah and Andy wanted peace in their chaotic lives. To accomplish that, a third party suggested that Sarah and Andy give their Christian neighbors their paychecks, charge cards, checkbook, and bills.

To do so, they had to trust somebody in addition to their neighbors. They had to believe that God would take care of their family. They had made a mess of it. Would they trust God to straighten it out?

They did. Although the money belonged to Sarah and Andy, his weekly check went next door. Their neighbors paid the bills, kept them on their budget, urged them to reconsider unnecessary purchases, and guided them to financial solvency. Now Andy and Sarah have their checkbook in their own pocket. They are out of debt. God controls their spending.

Once they learned that God would take care of them even if they gave up control of their spending, they were able to enjoy the game.

If we believe that the final score depends on the way we play the game, we'll never give up control. He promises us all we need if we seek him first. We'll only receive his promises when we give him control.

> *Once I understand that the final score is already in my favor, I'm left free to enjoy the good things he gives me.*

Notes

[1]Lloyd Cline Sears, *The Eyes of Jehovah—The Life and Faith of James Alexander Harding* (Nashville: Gospel Advocate, 1970), 43.

Focusing Your Faith:

1. How much of the stress in your life is money-
    related?

2. Describe the persons you admire because of the
    way they handle their money? Why do you
    respect them?

3. Do you think that Jesus would approve of saving
    accounts and retirement plans?

4. Does Jesus really expect us today to take Mat-
    thew 6:25-34 literally? Why?

5. Recall a time in your life when you knew without
    doubt that God unexpectedly provided for you.

6. How should the church be involved in the minis-
    try of helping each other learn how to manage
    money properly?

7. Would three of your closest friends agree that
    you control money or that money controls you?

Romans 6:1-14

What shall we say, then? Shall we go on sinning so that grace may increase? By no means! We died to sin; how can we live in it any longer? Or don't you know that all of us who were baptized into Christ Jesus were baptized into his death? We were therefore buried with him through baptism into death in order that, just as Christ was raised from the dead through the glory of the Father, we too may live a new life.

If we have been united with him like this in his death, we will certainly also be united with him in his resurrection. For we know that our old self was crucified with him so that the body of sin might be done away with, that we should no longer be slaves to sin—because anyone who has died has been freed from sin.

Now if we died with Christ, we believe that we will also live with him. For we know that since Christ was raised from the dead, he cannot die again; death no longer has mastery over him. The death he died, he died to sin once for all; but the life he lives, he lives to God.

In the same way, count yourselves dead to sin but alive to God in Christ Jesus. Therefore do not let sin reign in your mortal body so that you obey its evil desires. Do not offer the parts of your body to sin, as instruments of wickedness, but rather offer yourselves to God, as those who have been brought from death to life; and offer the parts of your body to him as instruments of righteousness. For sin shall not be your master, because you are not under law, but under grace.

Chapter 5

Leaving My Pretend World

∾

$\mathcal{I}$ used to pretend I was Roberto Clemente. He played for the Pittsburgh Pirates. I played in a sandlot. At the crack of the bat, Clemente leaped into action like a graceful deer covering the right field carpet in seconds, and then, just as the ball reached the top of the outfield fence, he would jump into the air, stretch out his arm, and catch the baseball in the web of his mit. When the bat cracked at Little League, my speed in right field came closer to that of a pregnant pig, and my last-minute jumps against the chain-link fence seldom caught the fly ball. But as I waddled across the field and hopped into the air, I imagined that I was the MVP right fielder for my beloved Pirates.

A visiting player's line drive toward the vine-covered wall at Forbes Field had no chance. Clemente would storm in from the warning track and in one fluid motion, reach down, scoop up the ball, and fire a strike to the first baseman. The umpire would throw his thumb into the air to the delight of all us Pirate fans. Line drives to right field

terrified me. After a momentary pause of disbelief
that the ball was actually coming my way, I would
drift over in the direction of the ball, lower my upper
body toward the coasting missile, extend my arm,
stab at the ball, watch it go by, and then run after it
as the batter rounded first. Even though I missed, I
still fantasized that I was Roberto Clemente.

About every third time at bat, Clemente would
drive a single to center field or whack one into the
upper deck in right. About every time at bat, I
struck out. I swung the bat like Clemente. I stood
deep in the batter's box like Clemente. I watched the
ball like Clemente. Somehow I conveniently ignored
the fact that, besides winning the batting title, my
hero also struck out more than any other Pirate.

My Little League coach played the other boys
more than he played me. Most of the time I sat on
the bench wondering why Clemente Junior wasn't on
deck. The other boys were in the real world, making
it to the major leagues (I never got out of the mi-
nors), while I spent all my time in the dream world
of the star right fielder for the Pirates.

I had another alter ego named Dan Newton.
Unlike Roberto Clemente, he didn't exist. He was
everything I wanted to be. Dan Newton owned a
huge farm, neatly kept, constantly expanding,
tremendously profitable, and always adventuresome.
When a crisis would erupt on the farm, Dan Newton
would race to the scene in his red pickup truck to
solve the problem. Dan was confident. I was uncer-
tain. Dan was a leader. I mostly followed. Dan was
aggressive. You could count on me to be pretty
passive. Dan liked his name in the headlines. I was
shy. He was successful. I thought of myself as a
clone of Roberto Clemente, yet deep inside I knew
that I was just no good at sports. Even though I

pretended to be he-has-it-all-together Dan Newton, I knew that I had a few pieces missing.

I'd go into the attic of our house, get out my toys, and for hours take on the form of Dan Newton. I never told anybody. In fact, until now, it's been my lifelong secret. I never wanted anybody to know that I wanted to be somebody else.

My two childhood heroes differed. One existed; the other did not. One was a baseball superstar, the other a farmer. One possessed superior ability, the other a superior character. I wanted to *do* what Clemente *did*, but I wanted *to be* what Dan Newton *was*. Sometimes we want to imitate the actions of others in our pretend worlds. Other times we want to be what other people are.

For most of us, pretending was part of childhood. After we pass a certain age, the pretending of childhood becomes the pretense of adult life. What once allowed us to expand our horizons and test our abilities creates in adulthood a person within a person, a face behind a face. We pretend to be what we are not. What others see is not what they get.

Two fundamental kinds of spiritual pretense exist. One is that we pretend to be alive when we're not. The second is that we feign our allegiance to God. Romans 6 discusses both kinds of pretense.

Pretending to Be Alive

Words associated with death occur eighteen times in Romans 6. Death has three different meanings in these twenty-three verses. First, it refers to the death of Jesus. Second, death describes our status if we reject God. Third, the word depicts our exit from the pretend world into the real world.

Our imaginary existence is one where we think

we can lick sin all by ourselves. The spiritual whopper deceives us into thinking that being good "depends on me." We've all gone through the routine: "I'm sorry, I won't do it again." "I've learned my lesson this time." "I don't know what in the world I was thinking when I did that." "If I can have one more chance, I think I can lick this." "I've put it on my list of New Year's Resolutions."

Pretending. That's all we're doing. We can dream about being the Roberto Clemente of sinlessness or the Dan Newton of holiness, but it's only a fantasy. Our dreams exceed our abilities: "I did it again." "I guess I didn't learn my lesson." "Déjà vu. I've done this before." "I thought I could lick it." "New Year's Resolutions? It's January 16. I've forgotten them already."

Romans 6 uses the word *death* to describe our exit from that pretend world. The text calls it a death to sin (6:2). Only pretenders maintain they need no help with sin. Those who die to sin recognize they need a higher power. God does what we could never do—he makes us good. We do not suddenly begin to master goodness by our own power, but God creates good in us. We do not suddenly act like better people, but someone makes us into better people. We do not engage in perfect self-improvement, but rather benefit in cross-centered improvement. Romans 6 calls that recognition a death. A death to an old way of thinking. A death to an old way of living. A death to an inferior pretend world.

Rescued from Death

Two dramas—one seen, one unseen—unfold as we die this death. The visible one is baptism. We act out what Jesus did. He died on a cross; we die to our pretend world. He was buried in a tomb; we are buried in a tomb of water. He arose from the grave on Resurrection Sunday; we come out of the watery grave with new life.

That drama unfolds on the stage whenever anyone accepts the grace of God in trusting faith. It's an impromptu action that takes place as we die to the pretend world. Baptism allows us to act out our faith. It reminds us and those who witness our death, of the death, burial, and resurrection that empowers our own transformation from pretend existence to the realm of reality.

Drama one takes place before a human audience. Drama two performs only to a heavenly assembly. The earthbound reenactment involves human hands and a depth of water. Drama two unfolds with heavenly hands and calls for depth of understanding.

The second drama features a marionette, the little jointed doll controlled by wires or strings on a miniature stage. The gaily dressed doll at the ends of the wires is manipulated by the person holding the other end of the wires. The doll jumps at the invisible controller's command, bows with the tip of his hand, waves with a movement of his thumb. The doll is his slave.

As the second drama begins, we find the arms tied to wires that extend into the sky. Somebody moves a wire and the head jerks. Another wire flexes and the right arm goes up and the left one goes down. We are the marionette. Sin sits at the controls. We think we run our lives, but we're really at the mercy of Sin. We're enslaved to Sin. Sin moves, we jerk. Sin lifts, we fly.

As we give up the pretend world, the figures on the second stage change places. A heavenly arm sweeps us off the stage, disconnects all the wires, puts the control to the wires in our hands and puts us in the area over the stage. As we look down we see that the other end of the wires are now attached to Sin. We move, Sin jerks. We lift, Sin flies.

The heavenly transformation of roles changes our life and the supernatural paradox begins. Sin no longer controls us, we control sin through the power of the cross. We're still on the stage with Sin, but its power over us has been broken because we have access to the power of Jesus' blood. Having died, we now live. Having given up the pretend world, we now exist in the real world. Death which once had dominion over us, pulling on our wires, now no longer has that power. Our roles have been switched. These two dramas occur at the same time. They bring us from death to life.

Pretending to Yield

Sometimes there's a problem. Sometimes the person reenacting the death, burial, and resurrection of Jesus in baptism hasn't given up the pretend world. Outwardly the first drama receives rave reviews. Only the actor or actress knows the deceit. Only the one baptized knows the pretense. The earthly audience sees no guile. But without the death of the pretend world, the second drama never unfolds. The wires remain attached to the marionette. The little doll still jumps to the movements of the hand of sin. The pretend world is still alive.

It's not unusual for people to sometimes question how much they understood about their engagement with the cross. Perhaps this text reaches out to those who know they are still pretenders. They were baptized to please the crowd, not to please God. They thought to themselves that they really didn't believe what was going on. They didn't really believe that

Jesus died on the cross, but responding was just the socially acceptable thing to do. They pretended.

They went through the right motions, but never sincerely intended to alter their lives.

They said the right words, but never committed to right living.

They went along with the crowd, but never gave themselves to Jesus.

I talked with a man last week who had "said the right things" and made the "right moves" but never died to sin. He told me: "I did what they told me to do because I wanted to be around those splendid people. Now, six months later, I've encountered Jesus. Now it's real. Now I come because he has changed my life."

Why does a book about giving control to God go back to conversion? No discussion of turning control over to God would be complete unless it went back to our first moment of surrender. Spiritual powerlessness may have its roots in a feigned death. Our inability to give God control of our lives may ultimately rest on the fiction that we submitted to him earlier in life.

How authentic was your death? Ask yourself:

- Do I live and act like I've been made alive, or do I live and act like I'm still dead?

- Do I speak like a person who has been set free, or do I talk like a slave?

- Do I have the joyful look of an acquitted person, or do I wear a look of guilt?

- Do I have the freedom of someone ransomed, or do I still act like I'm kidnapped?

- Do I live as if Christ did the work for me, or am I still trying to work my way into grace?

- Do I understand that he was sacrificed for me, or do I live in fear of the executioner?

Negative answers to the first part of each question call for a reexamination of the issues raised in Romans 6. Refusal to face our own sin can be a thinly disguised way of maintaining control. Thinking we're in control, we're actually dancing to Sin's commands. Romans 6 is the voice of reality calling us out of the pretend world.

Most likely you answered the first part of each question positively. That's confirmation that you've left the pretend world. You've given up the pretense that you can do it all by yourself. You've given up pretending to be as perfect as your childhood heroes. But that's not the end of the story. Romans 6 talks about a second kind of spiritual pretense.

Transformed into an Instrument of Righteousness

I've given up my childhood fantasy of being Roberto Clemente, so what else should I do? It's been years since I've pretended to be Dan Newton. If I've given up that pretend world, am I not in the real one?

Romans 6:13 (RSV) tells us:

Do not yield your members to sin as instruments of wickedness, but yield yourselves to God as men who have been brought from death to life, and your members to God as instruments of righteousness.

Because of the heavenly drama, I no longer have to submit to sin. I don't act on its stage. The wires that attached sin to my life have been cut. The strings that doomed me to slavery were snapped at the cross. Now I move on. I yield to God.

When we die to sin (Romans 6:1-11), but never

yield to God (Romans 6:12-14), we go through the door, but never live in the house. We register for school, but never go to class. We open the book, but never read the words.

Two things push us to yield. First, God calls us to yield because of our rescue from death. Once escorted out of the pretend world, we find ourselves so grateful that we willingly embrace God's world.

I was dead; now I'm alive. My transformation makes me want to jump up, fall down at his feet, and say, "Thank you. Use me."

> ***My transformation makes me***
> ***want to jump up, fall down at his***
> ***feet, and say, "Thank you. Use me."***

A doctor friend tells about doing successful surgery on a patient who was so grateful that he bought the physician a car. Rescue workers risk their lives to snatch a victim from death. Sometimes the grateful victim spends a lifetime repaying his saviors. Mildred Stutzman played a crucial role in bringing Christ into my life. Though gone now for several years, her picture on my shelf and her ministry in my heart keep her memory alive.

What happens in the two dramas provides good reason for yielding. Yet God entices me to yield in one other way. As he brings me from death to life, he makes me into an instrument of righteousness.

Instrument of righteousness? What's that? The words can also be translated as a "weapon of good" or as "tools for God."

As I yield, he makes me an instrument. I don't make myself into an instrument of righteousness.

He does. He uses me as an instrument. I become a
weapon in his hand, a tool used by God.

God does for me what my dream world could
never accomplish. I imagined I was the star Pittsburgh right fielder, but on my own I couldn't even
make it out of the minor leagues in third grade
sandlot baseball. I dreamed of being confident,
talented, polished Dan Newton, but even as a young-
ster I understood that my hero was everything I
wasn't. I could not do what I wanted to do, nor could
I be what I wanted to be.

Now God tells me I'm on his team. I become the
bat in God's hand. I become the equipment that he
uses. No longer in the minor leagues, I'm playing
with the maker of the world, the king of all kingdoms, the best of the best. No longer confined to
some red pickup on a well-kept farm, I'm with the
master farmer, with the personality of personalities,
filled with all his confidence and talent and polish.

I don't need to wait in line to sign up for a job; I'm
an instrument in God's hand. I don't have to go to boot
camp; I'm a weapon for good. I don't need to be sharpened; I'm a tool in the hand of God.

Living in a Dream World

Too many adults still fantasize being their version of Roberto Clemente or Dan Newton. Childhood
dream worlds become kingdoms of pretense as
adults. For people outside of Christ, it's the pretense
that I can make life what I want it to be. But I can't.
I won't.

Only when we die to that pretend world through
the spiritually simultaneous dramas of baptism and
salvation from sin do we find reality. Even so, people
inside of Christ often fail to yield to him. Dead to sin,

but not always an instrument of righteousness. Freed from the past, but sometimes unproductive in the present. Into the kingdom, but seldom settled down.

I remember my mother standing at the foot of the attic stairs.

"Harold? Harold! HAROLD!"

Pause.

"Harold, are you up there? Harold, answer me!"

Finally, her words penetrated through the windows of Dan Newton's shiny new pickup. Caught up in my fantasy, I didn't hear reality. Focused on my fictional heroes, I'd forgotten about real people. Only her persistent calling retrieved me from my pretend existence.

> *God calls us from the foot*
> *of the stairs. He tells us he's made*
> *us into weapons for good.*

God calls us from the foot of the stairs. He tells us he's made us into weapons for good. He yells up the stairs that we've been fashioned into his tools.

"You're an instrument of righteousness!"

Sometimes his words make us grip our fictional world more tightly. Sometimes the more he calls, the tighter we hold. The louder his voice, the deeper we dream. As his voice grows stronger, our distance grows greater.

As we retreat from God's voice, we also flee the knowledge that our reality falls short of our dream world. We think we can play life like Roberto Clemente played baseball. We believe we can be to our lives what Dan Newton was to our imagination. We forget that the harder we try to control life, the more it gets out of control. We hide in a dream world between the reality of our own failures and the prospect of God's willingness to renew us.

Our dream world allows us to believe the lie of all lies. Clemente made it happen. It all did depend on Dan Newton. If life depended on them, it must depend on me. In our dream world we're indispensable, we're in control. The barriers between the truth of dependence on God and the myth of self-dependency disappear in the land of fantasy.

In the dream world, we conveniently forget that living life successfully involves both giving up control and depending on God. In the fantasy world, we are the gods. We're the omnipotent ones. We're omnipresent. We create and sustain life on the Dan Newton ranch. We determine reality. We begin and end time in the pretend world. Nothing shatters fantasy like blood running down the cross. Nothing reminds us more that life is made up of giving up and depending on God than the life that Jesus lived.

Our fantasy world offers no surprises. We always catch the line drive. We always make money. We always get the promotion. We always come out on top. We control the fantasy world. Nothing offers more surprises to life than the God who pops the bubble of our pretend worlds.

Nobody keeps score in the pretend world. Counting runs reminds us too much of reality. Dream worlds offer no competition. We sweep the series. We get all the business. We top the charts. God offers wonderful assurance amid harsh realities. Nothing jerks us out of the pretend world more than keeping score. Only God can offer any predictions about the outcome of the game of life.

Our pretend world allows us to set aside our role as instruments of righteousness. Fantasizing prevents yielding. Pretending keeps us from surrendering.

The reality is that we've been created to yield. God knows that yielding leads to fulfillment. Yielding brings satisfaction. Yielding draws us into deep peace. Yielding allows us joy and happiness.

Two nine year olds sat in the minor league dugout at the sandlot off Oak Avenue. One boy imagined he was Roberto Clemente. The other tried to remember how his coach told him to hold the bat. One boy daydreamed of the ball going over the fence. The other kept repeating, "Keep your eye on the ball."

Emerging into Reality

I'd love to tell you sometime about the cold March day when I died to the old dream world and emerged into God's sunny reality. My baptism into Christ shattered that old imaginary world. Let me tell you instead about the day I yielded. Many of the students in my freshman class in college decided to go on the trip to Lubbock, Texas, to attend a seminar on world missions. It was a mixed group: business majors, athletes, pre-med students, girls looking for boys, boys looking for girls, some going with a clear sense of vision, others just on the bus for the ride.

Missionaries from around the world addressed the group pleading for students to commit themselves to either go or send. The cause of Christ beckoned us to take part. Former missionary Stanley Shipp offered the keynote address, calling us to commit to Christ. In a sense, he pointed out that some of us had died to the old life, but had never yielded ourselves to God. As we sang, I watched many of my friends move down the aisles as a statement that they had yielded themselves to God. Finally, I, too, realized that my commitment to God was incomplete.

I stepped out into the aisle.

College students often make incredible resolutions. Their belief in God's promises leads them to idealistic crusades and visionary goals. That night six of us gathered in one of the dorm rooms to pray about the future. Of all the people who had come on the bus to this workshop, we were the ones moved by the speaker's calling us to the Communist world. In 1968, the United States and the Soviet Union were locked in a bitter cold war and ideological struggle. We worried about the nuclear bomb. We feared that our children would be Communists. We felt our way of life was threatened. The six of us decided we'd be willing to be used by God to penetrate that world.

I was eighteen years old when the six of us knelt down and prayed honestly and tearfully that God would somehow use us in that venture. I prayed openly, but with a secret reservation that I would never see it happen. I was willing to yield myself, but never fully believed that God would honor that commitment or answer that prayer.

Twenty-five years later, I stood in Red Square outside the Kremlin telling people about Jesus. I preached dozens of times in the capital city of Ukraine. Person after person responded to Christ. I made friends with the very people who had always been my enemies. In my late thirties, God allowed me to fulfill a commitment made in my late teens.

Nothing changes one's perspective quite like yielding. By absolutely no effort of my own, I am an instrument of righteousness. Without any regard to my talents or abilities, I'm a tool of God. Although I have no training in military methods, God has used me as a weapon for good between two former enemies. Nothing looks the same after yielding to God. Being an instrument of righteousness affects the

way I hear, the things I see, the people I know.
Yielding makes me a different person in many ways:

- People at the mall are no longer fellow shoppers, but part of the mass of people dying in their pretend worlds.

- My house is no longer a retreat center for my private use, but a station used by God to welcome weary travelers.

- My sons are not chips off the old block, but temporary loans by God to train and disciple for his holy mission.

- My family is not just a supporting web of relationships to comfort me when I'm depressed or to cheer me up when I'm sad, but it is a unit aimed to give glory to God.

- The 168 hours each week are not mine to use up as I like, but moments in which God wields his weapons, grabs his tools, and sharpens his instruments.

- My limited amounts of energy are not like disposable income to meet my every whim, but are gifts of God to carry his message.

- The poor are not people to disown and frown on, or people to blame for high taxes and bad government, but they are special in God's sight.

- My money is not merely the resource on which to base my own comfort and luxury, but it is a tool in the hand of a tool, an instrument in the hand of God's instrument, a means of accomplishing God's work.

- The sick are not to be pitied and forgotten, but they are reminders of God's own suffering and of our interrelatedness as people.

When I imagined playing like Roberto Clemente and being like Dan Newton, I didn't know what God had in store. I didn't know that I would die to this world of sin and fantasy. I didn't know that, as I yielded to him, I would become an instrument in his hands. I didn't know about the cobblestones on Red Square or the cool breeze off Kiev's Dnieper River or the rotting timbers of America's decaying ghetto. All I know is that I'm glad I'm not pretending anymore.

> *Nothing offers more surprises to life*
> *than the God who pops the*
> *bubble of our pretend worlds.*

Focusing Your Faith:

1. Who is the person who played the most important role in leading you to Christ?

2. At what point in your spiritual journey did you realize you were truly being transformed by Christ?

3. Is it unrealistic to believe that we can actually share in Christ's death through baptism? On what basis do you believe this?

4. How does it make you feel to know that as a Christian, you have been empowered by God to overcome sin?

5. Refusal to face our own sin can be a disguised way of maintaining control. Why?

6. What difference does it make that God intends for you to be his tool of righteousness?

7. Identify at least three reasons why you struggle with yielding control to God. How can God help you in your struggle?

Deuteronomy 8:1-14

Be careful to follow every command I am giving you today, so that you may live and increase and may enter and possess the land that the LORD promised on oath to your forefathers. Remember how the LORD your God led you all the way in the desert these forty years, to humble you and to test you in order to know what was in your heart, whether or not you would keep his commands. He humbled you, causing you to hunger and then feeding you with manna, which neither you nor your fathers had known, to teach you that man does not live on bread alone but on every word that comes from the mouth of the LORD. Your clothes did not wear out and your feet did not swell during these forty years. Know then in your heart that as a man disciplines his son, so the LORD your God disciplines you.

Observe the commands of the LORD your God, walking in his ways and revering him. For the LORD your God is bringing you into a good land—a land with streams and pools of water, with springs flowing in the valleys and hills; a land with wheat and barley, vines and fig trees, pomegranates, olive oil and honey; a land where bread will not be scarce and you will lack nothing; a land where the rocks are iron and you can dig copper out of the hills.

When you have eaten and are satisfied, praise the LORD your God for the good land he has given you. Be careful that you do not forget the LORD your God, failing to observe his commands, his laws and his decrees that I am giving you this day. Otherwise, when you eat and are satisfied, when you build fine houses and settle down, and when your herds and flocks grow large and your silver and gold increase and all you have is multiplied, then your heart will become proud and you will forget the LORD your God, who brought you out of Egypt, out of the land of slavery.

Chapter 6

Love, Joy, and Peace Don't Pay the Bills

∽

My fingers felt like ice cubes. No, I wasn't at the fifty-yard line on a crisp November Saturday. We weren't sledding at the gully by Richland Elementary School. I wasn't changing a tire in the snow.

I was refinancing my house. I felt like I was writing with gloves on. Over and over I signed my name. With each signature, I felt my life slipping away.

The tedious voice of the young attorney next to me kept my focus on the pile of papers that awaited my chilled signature. He tried to render the stacked paragraphs of legalese into understandable street language without leaving himself open for a lawsuit. His attempts to warm up the room with humor about "acts of God" and the thicket of government regulations did little to lift the chill in my heart.

After translating four pages of small print into something like "You must agree to live in this house as your primary residence," he would point to a line for my chilled fingers to do their thing.

Five paragraphs boiled down to "You promise not to sue me for any mistakes I make."

Three pages of warnings reduced to "The bank can demand full payment at any time."

Two different documents came out saying: "The mortgage company can sell your loan to another company without your permission."

"The house is not in a flood plain."

"You will get termite protection."

"Hazard insurance has been purchased."

"Sign here." "Sign here." "Sign here."

Despite all the attempts at clarity, regardless of all the papers intent on keeping me informed, beyond the legal devices meant to protect the lawyer, the bank, and everybody else, I felt naked, vulnerable, and unprotected. The deal seemed so tightly sealed that nothing could go wrong. Yet I felt that each form stripped me of my defenses. Each unsteady signature strengthened the uncertainty in my heart. The chill in my fingers reminded me that each signature put me in greater danger of losing control. What if something goes wrong? Nothing I've signed protects me from losing my house. I could lose my good credit. If I sign this paper, I will owe this amount to somebody I've never met. Why don't they keep these rooms warmer?

Refinancing our house left me cold. I just hoped it wouldn't leave me out in the cold. After signing all those papers, I decided to look up the word mortgage. Nothing I read gave me much comfort.

Nothing in the history of the word warmed my soul. The first part of the word, mort, is French for "death." The last part, gage, means "promise."

Promise of death.

No wonder my fingers were so cold. I read on: The original idea held that if the borrower didn't pay, he said good-bye to his pledge. If the payments came in on time, the lender gave up claim to the pledge; it died to him. Somehow the explanation offered little comfort and did nothing for my cold fingers.

Each page snatches away my control. Every signature seems to strip away my privacy, my ownership, my control. The chill from my fingers comes from the coldness in my heart.

God seems so far away at such times. At times like house closings or purchasing a car, I feel an odd estrangement from my faith. We pray for healthy children, for safe vacations, and for job security, but nobody ever seems to pray about a good house closing. God provides me with joy, but I sense it only after the mortgage payment is safely in the mail. God brings peace, but peace doesn't pay the bills.

Only money pays the bills. Only making the payment on time keeps the snipping dogs of foreclosure or repossession at bay. Financial security depends on cash flow. More cash equals greater security. Greater security means more control.

Bring on the cash.

Nothing warms my cold fingers like hot cash. Nothing covers the nakedness I feel at closing more than the finely woven texture of greenbacks. Nothing protects me from the vulnerability of monthly payments, nothing delivers me from the curse of credit card payments, nothing frees me to live like I want to like a healthy group of numbers at the bottom of my bank statement.

Bring on the cash.

I'm all for love, joy, and peace. But only hard U.S. currency pays the bills. Talk all day about discipleship and godliness, but you can't do without dollars. God has yet to offer mortgage loans at a lower rate than the local savings and loan. Count on me being at church, but don't ask me to give up my wallet.

Bring on the cash.

Yet my ice-cubed fingers remind me of my fears. Why doesn't money warm my soul? Maybe the greatest truth about finances is tied up in the phrase "cold cash." Why do I feel all alone? Is there any assurance that God works even when we put our financial future on the line?

Whom Do You Trust?

Let me tell you about another real estate transaction recorded in Deuteronomy 8. It wasn't the typical closing with buyers, sellers, and attorneys sitting around a walnut table in a chilly room. The buyers all stood. The sellers didn't appear. The only papers were the ones being used to record the speech. Nobody had yet heard of a closing attorney.

Moses' speech talks about the business of Israel. Although they do not have a lawyer overseeing the closing on their new property in Canaan, Moses covers each item on the business page by discussing three case studies.

Case Number One

Suppose there is a place where you have nothing. Imagine a place stripped of all financial amenities. Think of a spot where you can't pull yourself up by the bootstraps. Think of a place where you have no job. There is no benevolent government to provide a financial safety net. Nobody owns any land. Nobody owns a house. Each day you move to a new location. The soil has more sand and rocks than fertility and moisture. You have no neighbors. There are no banks or financial institutions within five hundred miles.

What would happen in a situation like that? Would God provide? Would life be threatened?

When Moses gave his Deuteronomy 8 speech at the closing on their new land, he reminded them that such a situation had occurred during the forty years in the wilderness. "When you had nothing, when you didn't even have food for breakfast, what did you learn?"

Not a sound went through the crowd at closing as they thought back over four decades of living with nothing. Suddenly, they looked at the years in the wilderness as a whole. Realization of what God had done filled their hearts. Without any international aid, without one shekel spent on food, a nation survived conditions worse than a famine. They looked down at their feet to see that they were wearing the same Egyptian shoes that their parents wore crossing the Red Sea forty years earlier. They felt the shirt stretched over their backs and remembered the loom next to the Nile that had made the fabric for their parents nearly a half century before. They remembered the gullies and the snakes, the sharp rocks and the spiders, but nobody could recall having a bruise or a broken arm, a swollen foot or an aching head.

The financial realities of the first case study in Deuteronomy 8:2-5 astounded the crowd. Without any effort on their part, they survived. Life in the desert was not heaven. Were they ever hungry? Yes. Were they ever thirsty? Yes. Were they always comfortable? No. Did they ever face danger? Yes. Did people die? Yes.

Yet the desert experience pointed to a financial truth: The people survived without money. The issue between God and his people is not shoe leather or finances. The question is not bread or business. The point is not about manna or industry.

There was no K-Mart along any Sinai highway.

Sand dunes don't charge rent. There was no meter on the water that came out of the rock. The pillar of fire that directed their journey sent out no bills. The issue is not bring on the cash.

The issue is God.

Case Number Two

God doesn't always deliver bread every morning like he did in the wilderness. Not all shoes come with indestructible soles. Not all nomads have access to such durable fabrics. The second case study in Deuteronomy 8:7-10 describes a different financial setting. Look at the financial resources given to a second group of people:

1. Fertile land;
2. Good sources of fresh water;
3. Operational water system;
4. Developed flood control;
5. Irrigation equipment for higher elevations;
6. Healthy wheat fields;
7. Prosperous barley crop;
8. Extensive vineyards;
9. Productive fig orchards;
10. Developed pomegranate industry;
11. Operational olive production;
12. Honey facilities;
13. Abundant staples and consumer goods;
14. Iron mining establishment;
15. Capacity for production and utilization of copper and related metals.

What financial team put together such a great place? Which business school is responsible for the theoretical thinking that led to such economic bliss?

Should we bring on the cash?

No economic cartel buried the natural resources in the ground. No agribusiness created such fertile soil. No dredging corporation put in the water system. AAA Plumbing didn't set up the springs. No human hand created the honeybee.

"The LORD your God gave it to you."

The text is clearly talking economics. This is about ownership, about money, about business, about prosperity, about growth, about fertility, about markets. The God who seems so distant from the mortgage closing provided some spectacular numbers in Deuteronomy 8.

And what an odd turnabout. Slaves who ate their bread off the ground for forty years in the wilderness now move into four-room houses complete with courtyards in Canaan. A man wearing forty-year-old shoes takes charge of the third shift in the world's largest copper mine. The woman who cooked manna over an open fire in the wilderness now has pomegranates on the table and olive oil on the shelf. A nation which could scarcely find bread for four decades now has bread without scarcity. This is not one person out of 51 million winning the state lottery; this is an entire nation of people moving from the slums to the suburbs.

What's the point? Put up with the desert, and you'll get your dessert? Eat manna for forty years, and I'll make it worth your while? Good things come to those who wait?

Those conclusions miss the way the finger points. If all we see is the glitter of Palestine, the bull market in Jerusalem, or the opportunity of an expanding economy, we've missed the reason for the speech. The finger is not pointing at the land or at the abundance or at the industry.

The finger points at God.

This speech at the closing on the promised land contains a bit more than just the case studies. The text is structured like a Big Mac sandwich with an extra layer: bread, *meat*, bread, *meat*, bread, *meat*, bread. The three case studies are the meat.

The four pieces of bread repeat the same message. Take the top piece of bread for example:

> Be careful to follow every command I am giving you today, so that you may live and increase and may enter and possess the land that the LORD promised on oath to your forefathers (Deuteronomy 8:1).

The speaker hits the same point in all four bread slices (Deuteronomy 8:1, 6, 11, 18-20). The common refrain in the chapter links it together, pointing out the connection between God and finance in terms of a challenge and a promise. God challenges the people to follow him. If they do, the financial underpinning of society is guaranteed.

Yet the theme of the chapter goes beyond just keeping the rules. It's not simply a matter of blindly following the commandments. The issue is control. God wants to know if the people understand that they don't live by bread (economics) alone, but by the word of God—giving control to God (Deuteronomy 8:3). That's what the wilderness was about.

So right in the middle of the closing proceedings on their new land, God stops the financial transaction to ask, "Who's in control?" In the middle of the biggest business deal in Israelite history, God slows the process long enough to raise the most crucial economic question ever put to a spiritual community: "Who runs this show?"

Now comes the climax.

Case Number Three

In Case Number One, Moses describes a situation where people have nothing, while Case Number Two presents a profile of abundance. Case Number Three builds on the second case study. What happens to people from the desert who move into a prosperous land? What problems do folks develop when their bank accounts grow and their stock holdings multiply? What happens to the heart when the streets are lined with nice houses? What takes place within the consumer when the stores are filled with nice things? What happens when the business section is filled with rosy graphs and reports of big dividends?

Case Number Three answers those questions. When prosperity comes to town, the people caught up in the parade think they are the grand marshal. They trust their own power to get what they want. They begin to think that they are alone in this financial world with nobody to help them.

The Bible's biggest "beware" is stated right here: "Beware lest you say in your heart, 'My power and the might of my hand have gotten me this wealth'" (Deuteronomy 8:17, RSV).

Ironic. The slaves think they built Jerusalem. The nomads take credit for the market. Cushy circumstances make us forget the real world.

The text calls us to forget for a moment all the equipment that weighs down our financial ships. Cast all these things out of your mind for just a minute:

- Your bank balance;
- Your credit card debt;
- The tax forms in the top desk drawer;
- The remaining years on your mortgage;
- All the things you'd like to have someday.

Forget the whole package. Forget the cold fingers at signing. Forget the prospect of losing your house. Forget the business of tomorrow morning. Focus on these questions:

- Who's in control?
- Whom do you trust?
- Who has the power?
- Who calls the shots?

One word summarizes the twenty verses of Deuteronomy 8—control.

Trust in God

We think the fundamental business question of life is, "Can God be trusted to take care of us financially?" Deuteronomy refocuses us by asking, "Can we keep our faith regardless of the finances?"

The chief issue behind finances is not whether God is in control. That's not what finances are about. Finances test us. Finances raise the question of how clearly we see, not how faithful God is. Affluence and poverty make us come clean about where we stand with God, not where God stands with us.

The question is never whether God is in control. The issue is whether or not we recognize that he is.

I opened the chapter with an issue that seemed to be at spiritual loose ends: God's apparent distance at my mortgage closing. Deuteronomy 8 helped me tie up those loose ends. God stands behind financial transactions. God is not absent. We just haven't tried to see him. Since we typically think we're in financial central, God gets pushed off the ledger. People who've only known Case Study Two of living in prosperity often end up as Case Study Three, thinking they are financially independent. Since few of us personally experience the wilderness, God's constant refrain of the relationship between financial control and faith reminds us of our constant need in financial matters to keep faith in God and leave control to God.

Yet if you've read carefully, you've noticed that two things about this financial analysis don't add up. One is that giving up control to God does not free us from economic decisions. Deuteronomy 8:18 makes it clear that God puts the potential to acquire wealth in our hands. We can invest a dollar and end up with two. We can waste a dollar and end up with none.

The question is never whether God is in control. The issue is whether or not we recognize that he is.

Stephen Covey's The Seven Habits of Highly Effective People draws a helpful distinction in the business world that applies to Deuteronomy 8. He argues for a difference between leaders and managers. He cites a common definition:

Management is doing things right; leadership is doing the right things. Managers get the business up the ladder. Leadership makes sure the ladder leans against the right wall. Managers cut the path through the jungle. Leadership makes sure the path goes in the right direction.[1]

God leads. God controls. God picks the wall. God sets the direction.

We manage. We set up schedules. We route the paperwork. We set up policies to achieve his goals.

Deuteronomy 8 issues no call to quit the business world. It offers no critique on making money. It shuts down no industry. But it does call us to give leadership to God.

The other financial issues loom more seriously. Sometimes God doesn't appear to be in financial control. People in the world do starve to death. Sometimes Christian people go without food. Missionaries report hardships experienced by people from underdeveloped countries. How can we square poverty with God's control of the business world? Can we trust a God who lets some people starve? That's the subject of the next chapter.

Nothing makes the blood flow through my fingers any better than releasing my grip. As manager, I sign the papers at closing. God gives me the right to make choices. He won't prevent me from making foolish purchases or wasting my money, but he does guarantee that I live by faith and not merely by my own financial ability.

God will lead our finances when we allow him to. Sometimes I see it. Sometimes, buried in mounds of paperwork or confronted by legal forms to sign, I miss it. Maybe my cold fingers served a purpose after all. They reminded me to keep my heart warm toward God. Deuteronomy 8 helps me see the connection between cold hands and a warm heart. The icy fingers remind me that God's control is the only way to keep the chill from invading my heart.

> *Affluence and poverty make us come clean about where we stand with God, not where God stands with us.*

Notes

[1]Stephen Covey, *The Seven Habits of Highly Effective People* (New York: Simon & Schuster, 1989), 100-03.

Focusing Your Faith:

1. Share a time in your life when you know that God helped you financially.

2. Should we expect God to do for us the same types of surprising things he did for the children of Israel? Why?

3. How often do you consult God about your financial decisions? Give an example.

4. Why can prosperity be more devastating than poverty to someone (Deuteronomy 8:17)?

5. Think of a personal financial struggle you fear most. Answer these questions in Case Number Three: Who's in control? Whom do you trust? Who has the power? Who calls the shots?

6. Giving up control does not free us from economic decisions. What economic decisions have you made which honor God's control of your finances?

7. Deuteronomy 8 causes us to ask, "Can we keep our faith regardless of the finances?" How is God strengthening your faith through your current financial circumstances?

Psalm 82:3

Defend the cause of the weak and fatherless;
maintain the rights of the poor and oppressed.

Isaiah 1:17

Learn to do right!
Seek justice,
encourage the oppressed.
Defend the cause of the fatherless,
plead the case of the widow.

Luke 6:36

Be merciful, just as your Father is merciful.

James 1:27

Religion that God our Father accepts as pure and faultless is
this: to look after orphans and widows in their distress and to
keep oneself from being polluted by the world.

Chapter 7

God's
Care-Package Plan

‿◌⁀

$\mathcal{T}$ears and fire.

That's the way I felt. Tears because I pitied the poor child. Tears because one of my boys was her age. Tears because of the blood.

Fire because I hated what was being done. Fire because it was unfair and cruel. Fire because I was angry about the blood.

It happened at a carpet factory on the muddy side of the Nile in Egypt. Guides often brought the tour groups to the two-story buildings set up to catch the pity of the American tourist with the hopes of making money. Each rug had a clearly written price in dollars. The memory I could not blot out was the cost in children.

A bus ride through Cairo takes the traveler into the heart of the third world. An ancient cemetery has become a huge slum. Squatters live in the mausoleums. Families eat on tombstones. Children play among the dead. Huge piles of first-world trash become the supermarkets for third-world mothers. You can't turn your head away. It's everywhere.

The carpet stores sell rugs to foreign tourists, and the proposed rationalization is clear. Either the children work here, or they sift through the garbage piles. Eight year olds get their education from reading tombstones, or they learn English from the never-ending line of tourists stepping off their air conditioned buses.

The little eight-year-old girl with the dark Egyptian complexion and the long black hair worked her shuttle near the door of the basement carpet factory. She had the good spot. She was first to be seen, first to be pitied.

When the guide turned away, she pointed to a dirty greenback in her hand. Weaving wasn't her only occupation. She also had a bachelor's degree in begging. When the guide turned back, she sent the shuttle singing through the loom. However many times she had disguised her begging without a hitch, it didn't work this time. The edge of the thread tied to the shuttle caught the side of her finger. Blood squirted out. She quickly moved the hand away so she wouldn't spoil the carpet. Somehow she kept weaving with the one hand while trying to stop the flow of blood with the other hand.

The price tag said $800. I knew better than that.

My eight year old concerns himself with computer games and soccer strategy. His biggest problem is how to get through supper without eating lima beans. The eight-year-old weaver works for the carpet store owner and for the tourist dollar. I suspect her biggest problem is getting supper.

Life Isn't Fair

Life is not fair. The unjust distribution of wealth may be more apparent in Cairo or New Delhi than in

Memphis or Houston, but we do not live in a fair world. We face constant reminders of life's inequities:

- Television reports about starving children on the barren plains of Africa;
- News leaking out of nations in Southeast Asia about concentration-camplike settings where lives mean nothing;
- Families standing next to the mall entrance with their cardboard sign: "Will work for food";
- Earthquakes in the third world claiming more lives than the population of small cities;
- Glimpses of blood-stained children caught in the battlefields of Israel or Sarajevo or Ireland.

God Promises Protection

Our question boils down to this: How can a God who claims to be in control allow this to happen? Why give up control to a God who can't keep the world under control?

God gives a three-part defense. It won't do any good to hear just part of it. It comes as a package deal. In fact, nothing may challenge our notion of control more than the answer God gives about the eight-year-old weaver in the Cairo slums.

The little girl with the bloody finger seems so helpless. Her life seems as vulnerable to a corrupt world as her skin does to the rough edge of the carpet yarn. Ethiopians stand in lines a mile long waiting to get the only food available to them. Orphan children in Sarajevo beg to be adopted. Do they stand alone?

On the following pages I will present three sets of Bible verses that reveal God's care-package plan. Each set will cite a passage from each of these four

books of the Bible: Psalms, Isaiah, Luke, and James.
The choice of these four is not arbitrary. They cover
the spectrum of theological offering in Scripture.

The Psalms, Israel's songbook, offer us comfort.
They provide God-inspired words that inspire us to
speak to God. God's defense of his control finds its
roots in this book of worship.

Isaiah presents the Bible in miniature. Isaiah's
66 chapters reflect the Bible's 66 books. The first 39
chapters talk about God's work in the past, just as
the Old Testament's 39 books reflect on the long
history of God's efforts. The last 27 chapters of
Isaiah deal with the coming of a glorious servant
and the nature of his work. The 27 books of the New
Testament tell of Jesus and his church. Just as the
Bible claims to be the inspired words of God, Isaiah's
central point is to call people to "hear the word of the
Lord." Rooted at the core of the biblical message is a
word about God's control.

Luke presents the life of Jesus who ministered to
the rich Zacchaeus (chapter 19) and to the poor,
maimed, lame, and blind (chapter 14). His mother
celebrated his birth by telling of his work among the
poor (1:46-56). Jesus embraced a ministry that
celebrated God's control over the rich and the poor.

James, the New Testament Proverbs, gives
practical directions for walking with Jesus. From
angry words to the virtue of patience, James tells us
how to be friends with God (4:4). It's a call to be in
relationship with a God who is in control.

First Defense: Tree of Refuge

To us, the little weaver in Cairo and the poor man
outside the shopping mall represent God's lack of
control in the world. All four books disagree. God,
they say, is the refuge for the little girl, the man,

and all the world's poor.

The Lord is a refuge for the oppressed, a stronghold in times of trouble (Psalm 9:9).

You have been a refuge for the poor, a refuge for the needy in his distress, a shelter from the storm and a shade from the heat (Isaiah 25:4).

Blessed are you who are poor, for yours is the kingdom of God (Luke 6:20).

Listen, my dear brothers: Has not God chosen those who are poor in the eyes of the world to be rich in faith and to inherit the kingdom he promised those who love him? (James 2:5).

Did you catch the thread that weaves itself through those four passages? From Old Testament to New Testament, from book of worship to book of guidance, from the master prophet to the last prophet, the message is the same. God is the refuge for the poor.

It's one thing to say that the eight-year-old girl with the bleeding finger has a refuge in God, and another thing to do something for her. How do we know that this refuge business is serious? Listen to the "crayon man."

"Crayon man" is one description applied to Harvard psychiatrist Robert Coles, who spent the last couple of decades studying children in America. With a piece of construction paper and a box of crayons, he sits down to talk to kids. In one of his books, he talks to poor kids. Expecting to find their attitudes as poor as their pocketbooks, he found the exact opposite. It was among the poor that he found faith, hope, and courage. In richer homes he encountered boredom and alienation, not the happiness and bliss he expected.

What Coles found in America, missionaries have reported around the world. The most rapid spread of the Christian faith in recent times has come in the third world countries in Southeast Asia, central Africa, and Latin America. In 1993, nearly 30,000 Chinese converted to some kind of Christian church each day. There were no Protestant churches in South Korea at all in 1900. Today nearly a third of South Koreans embrace some form of evangelical faith. Protestants in Vietnam numbered about 100,000 in 1975. Fifteen years after the American soldiers and missionaries left the war-torn land, the churches report nearly 300,000 members. According to missionaries I've talked to, the area of the world with the most rapid growth is the poor, tribal areas of Kenya, where dozens of new churches have been planted in recent years.

Faith flourishes in the world's ghettos and food lines.

The poor have faith in God because they have no means of control, they have no money to manage, and they have no investment to protect. It's a peculiar blessing that God offers the poor. They give up control and put faith in God with greater ease than those of us who have a stash to guard or who nurture a culture of control. Faith flourishes in the world's ghettos and food lines.

God's refuge comes by way of faith. His cool shade for a scorched world comes in the form of hope for people in depressing situations. But God's protective arm goes further, as revealed in the second set of Scriptures.

Second Defense: Key to Hope

She may not know it, but God makes tremendous promises to the eight-year-old carpet weaver. To people in her situation, who lived when the pyramids were thousands of years younger and to people not yet born, God offers these vows:

> "Because of the oppression of the weak and the groaning of the needy, I will now arise," says the LORD. "I will protect them from those who malign them" (Psalm 12:5).

> Is not this the kind of fasting I have chosen: to loose the chains of injustice and untie the cords of the yoke, to set the oppressed free and break every yoke (Isaiah 58:6)?

> He has brought down rulers from their thrones but has lifted up the humble (Luke 1:52).

> Now listen, you rich people, weep and wail because of the misery that is coming upon you. Look! . . . The wages you failed to pay the workmen who mowed your fields are crying out against you. The cries of the harvesters have reached the ears of the Lord Almighty (James 5:1, 4).

These four verses carry a common message. Like a train loaded with iron ore, each verse supplements the others:

- God will protect the poor;
- God will correct the injustice and remove the chains;
- God will depose oppressive rulers;
- God listens to the cries of the oppressed.

God provides refuge. He protects the poor flock

under his wing in faith. But God goes beyond just a
warm place of security by promising to correct the
injustice and to right the wrong. What do all these
promises mean to the poor in American ghettos or to
the starving in Ethiopia or the families still bearing
the bruises of war and disaster in Southeast Asia?
We need some special tools to understand how these
promises work.

All sorts of things get piled up in our small workshop next to the garage. There's the toaster waiting
for a new plug. A small napkin holder awaits paint.
Wood for shelving in the family room needs cutting.
The project my eight year old and I worked on last
month needs assembly. Projects in stages of incompleteness don't bother me. I understand how some
things have to wait to dry, others need sanding, that
certain kinds of craft cannot be rushed. My son is
less patient. Most projects we do together cover a
fairly short time span. He wants to cut, assemble,
glue, sand, paint, and varnish—all in one Saturday
afternoon. One of the primary tools of any good
workshop is patience. Sharpened blades, gluing
clamps, and clean brushes mean little if the tool of
patience hangs on the rack.

One of the primary tools of
any good workshop is patience.

When it comes to this recent collection of verses, I
feel like I'm in God's workshop. Some of his projects
await paint. Some need cutting out. Others only
need assembly. His timing baffles me as much as my
timing escapes my eight year old. Nothing troubles
me more than God's slow response to the poor. God

recently taught me a lesson about his timing. It wasn't in my workshop, but in my office.

Ream Mom keeps our church building in top shape, and he often steals into my office to empty the trash or tidy up. Sometimes he walks so quietly I don't realize he's there until I catch sight of his shadow on my computer monitor. By then, I'm almost hiding behind his shadow. Last fall, when he tapped me on the shoulder, he almost sent me through my computer screen. Rather than coming to clean, he tiptoed in to share.

Ream grew up in Cambodia, working the rice paddies on the family farm. War in Southeast Asia ripped that pleasant, agricultural life to shreds. Communist sympathizers made life difficult. They imprisoned and tortured Ream, who survived only because his wife, Yun, slipped him food. While Ream watched for her daily deliveries, he saw the guards kill Yun's sister. Finally Ream escaped, gathered up all the family members he could find, and headed toward the border. Ream led his family out of their homeland by swimming the Mekong River. With two babies in tow, they made the wet journey to freedom.

Circumstances forced them to leave their four-year-old daughter behind.

Moving from one refugee camp to another, the Moms found something they didn't expect. This Buddhist family learned about Jesus. As they moved, they longed to begin life again. A relative in the United States led them to appeal to some Christians in Memphis, Tennessee. The long flight for freedom ended at the Memphis International Airport. After settling in, both Ream and Yun started working at our church building. Each day their English improved. They bought their own home and purchased a Chevy station wagon.

In July 1992 Ream and Yun stood before a federal judge to be sworn in as American citizens. The following Sunday their church family rejoiced in their victory.

With American citizenship, Ream and Yun could return to Cambodia without fear of being detained. They took vacation time to go back home.

While Ream and Yun lived in America, their four-year-old daughter grew up in Cambodia. She married a young man, and two years ago she gave birth to Ream and Yun's first grandson. Last summer Ream met Pisit Kim; grandpa met grandson.

Ream brought the pictures directly from Fox Photo to the office. He came to share the pictures; he came to share the joy. Grandfather and grandson at the park. Grandfather and grandson on the floor. Ream and Pisit at the market. A family reunited.

But for me Ream brought an even bigger picture. He brought the promises from Psalms-Isaiah-Luke-James into focus. In one man's life, God had kept his word. He felt Ream's oppression. He lifted up the humble. He unlocked the prison doors; he broke every yoke.

The smile on Ream's face and the joy in his heart about Pisit told me something about the mysterious hand behind all the bloody wars, beyond all the barbed-wire fences, and deep within the Mekong River. In the life of one man, God had sent justice. In the life of one family, God had removed the chains.

But it seems like too little, too late. Why Ream and Yun, and not the thousands of others who perished in Southeast Asia? Like my eight year old's impatience with my six-month project, I grow weary of waiting for God to assemble his plan of justice. Then I look at pictures of Pisit and remember a different story.

Third Defense: A Cooperative Effort

The story about God's control of the poor has three points. So far, we've looked at two.

God is the shade tree for a thirsty world—he is our refuge. God is the key that opens the prison doors—he keeps his promises. Beyond tree and key, God does one more thing. He calls us to help free the oppressed.

'Look at the third point made by the four biblical books:

Defend the cause of the weak and fatherless; maintain the rights of the poor and oppressed (Psalm 82:3).

Learn to do right! Seek justice, encourage the oppressed. Defend the cause of the fatherless, plead the case of the widow (Isaiah 1:17).

Be merciful, just as your Father is merciful (Luke 6:36).

Religion that God our Father accepts as pure and faultless is this: to look after orphans and widows in their distress and to keep oneself from being polluted by the world (James 1:27).

Imperatives shoot out of the biblical texts from four different periods of history. Commands to the faithful of all generations. Demands for assistance. A call to arms. Involvement of the spiritual community in the cause of right for the God who is in control.

Verses like these make me wish I had my remote control. I'll just change to a different channel. If the book of Psalms is going to tell me to help the poor, I'll switch to something else. Let me see what's on the Isaiah channel. Click.

Oh, no, more stuff on the poor. Let me try the Gospel channel. Jesus brings me grace and mercy.

Let me hear a good parable. Click.

More stuff on the poor. James is just the practical book I need to hear. Give me something I can chew on, James.

Click. More stuff on the poor.

Click. The sound of control. The sound of a closed mind. The sound of the mind that wants to be master. Whenever I'm challenged to help the poor, I gravitate toward control. I don't want to do it. Helping the disenfranchised, the underprivileged, means doing what I don't want to do. It means bowing to the will of a higher power. It brings me face to face with my own insecurity by making me wonder what fate of life put me in one place and them in another. Not only do I not want to help, I can tell you why. I've got a lot of good reasons for not helping the poor:

- If the poor didn't have so many babies, they wouldn't be poor.
- If third-world countries didn't have so much corruption, they wouldn't be poor.
- Poor people are lazy. They just don't want to work.
- The government should take care of the down and out. That's their job.
- We already send foreign aid. That ought to be enough.
- If they would manage their money better, they wouldn't be in this fix.

Do you have some you'd add to the list? I bet you do. We control people can think of a host of reasons not to help the poor.

Add to the list. Write your reasons for not helping the poor in the margin. Flip over to the back of the book and find a blank page. Get a legal pad and fill it up. Get it out of your system. When you've got all the reasons out, read the next two paragraphs.

We use the eight year old in Cairo as evidence that God is not in control. We refuse to help the down and out because we want to stay in control.

God uses the eight year old in Cairo as evidence that he is in control. God calls us to help the down and out as a means of recognizing his control.

> *God calls us to help the down and out as a means of recognizing his control.*

Let me make God's challenge to you crystal clear. Find some people who are down and out. Get to know them. Get close to them. Find out what's inside. Learn about why they live the way they do.

I guarantee you'll learn two things:

1. You are like them in more ways than you ever dreamed;
2. You have less control over your life than they do over theirs.

In the process of visiting with those unfortunate people, you will learn more about control than I could ever tell you. You will understand that it was not just for the sake of the poor that God calls us to help the oppressed. It is for us. God calls his people to show compassion to the unfortunate because it enriches life. God demands that we stand for justice because it clarifies our existence. God asks us to help free the world's trapped people because it may be the most freeing exercise of our life. God calls us to join him in his crusade for justice to flow like waters and for righteousness to roll like a never-ending stream.

Because nothing else in our experience will draw us closer to God and his plan than being on his side in an unfair and unjust world.

Ream and I shared his victory. Though I've never been in a Communist prison like Ream, helping him start a new life has given me a greater taste of freedom. Seeing Ream's joy at meeting young Pisit made me see a whole new way of experiencing joy.

Every visit to one of our inner city housing projects, every bottle of medicine I've given to children with cancer in Ukraine, and every homeless job training lab graduation I've attended have, in some way, helped a person on the downside of life. But in the process, I have gained a degree of understanding of the God who controls me and the world.

The little eight-year-old carpet weaver represents one of God's special people. The poor and oppressed are everywhere. They are a test—a life exam to see whether we are up to giving up control. They confront us with the ultimate trial: Will we submit to God?

> *God asks us to help free the world's trapped people because it may be the most freeing exercise of our life.*

Focusing Your Faith:

1. Think of a time when you felt the pain of life's injustice. How did your response honor or dishonor God?

2. Looking back in this chapter, locate the Bible verses that best reveal God's care package of refuge and hope. Why do these verses give you the most comfort?

3. Why is it much easier to *believe* that God is our refuge than it is to live out that belief?

4. When you are in despair, what comforting Scripture or song comes to your mind?

5. If the "crayon man" were to sit down with you, would he see a picture of faith, hope, and courage, or discouragement, despair, and fear?

6. What insight about God's timing did you learn from Ream Mom's struggle against oppression?

7. Imagine you have brought home two street people as dinner guests. Are you feeling joy or anxiety? Why?

Isaiah 40:27-31

Why do you say, O Jacob,
and complain, O Israel,
*"My way is hidden from the L*ORD*;*
my cause is disregarded by my God"?
Do you not know?
Have you not heard?
*The L*ORD *is the everlasting God,*
the Creator of the ends of the earth.
He will not grow tired or weary,
and his understanding no one can fathom.
He gives strength to the weary
and increases the power of the weak.
Even youths grow tired and weary,
and young men stumble and fall;
*but those who hope in the L*ORD
will renew their strength.
They will soar on wings like eagles;
they will run and not grow weary,
they will walk and not be faint.

Jeremiah 12:5

If you have raced with men on foot
and they have worn you out,
how can you compete with horses?
If you stumble in safe country,
how will you manage in the thickets
by the Jordan?

Chapter 8

Living in the Heights

∽

The worn cover and soiled pages of my *Roget's International Thesaurus* reflect its constant use. With nearly a quarter million English words, it helps me find the ones I want. Some of the entries have little brackets after them. For example, the list of synonyms for *assent* includes two words with brackets: "O.K. [slang]; give thumbs up [colloquial]."

Instead of the formal word *assent* most of us use the slang expression "O.K.," or in some parts of the English speaking world we say "give it thumbs up."

In all my years of using my friend Roget, one list seems to have more brackets than any other: Entry 715, *fatigue.* Notice these unusual synonyms:

- tired [chiefly dialect]
- tuckered [colloquial, U.S.]
- frazzled [chiefly U.S.]
- tuckered out [colloquial, U.S.]
- pooped out [slang]
- used up [colloquial]

- bushed [slang]
- pegged out [slang]
- beat-up [slang]
- used up [slang]
- seedy [colloquial]
- washed-up [colloquial]
- done in [slang]
- dead [colloquial]

That's quite a motley crew that we English speakers use to tell others about our exhaustion. I know I've been bushed, tuckered out, and done in, but I never have described myself as beat-up or seedy.

Weary and Worn

Whether we say we're tuckered out or just dead, we know the feeling. Sometimes it's weariness from hard physical labor. Putting in too many hours will also bring it on. Having too many things to do in a certain period leads to this common malady. Even sheer boredom or dull routine makes us feel used up. But several times recently, I've just been beat:

- The day we put in the sidewalk around the garage to the backyard.
- The 23-hour trip from Ukraine to Memphis.
- A seven-mile hike down the Wolf River Trails (why didn't we turn back earlier?).
- Ninety minutes of racquetball with the class A guys.
- Cleaning the attic (and resulting garage sale).
- Running alongside my six year old trying to teach him how to ride his bike.

Aching muscles. Short attention spans. Hallucinations about bed. Calloused hands. All of it comes with fatigue.

Mental Fatigue

But there's another kind of weariness that doesn't go away. After a few days, the fatigue generated by transforming the three yards of concrete into a sidewalk will disappear. Three games of racquetball doubles stay in the memory as something not to do again, but the muscles quickly rebound. There's another kind of weariness that exists in the mind.

- Weariness about a job that doesn't pay the bills and only burdens our soul.
- Exhaustion with the mediocre nature of life.
- Tired because we find nothing to inspire us, to excite us, to engage our minds.
- Worn out with the dullness of the daily routine.
- Fatigued by opposition and resistance.
- Strained by the sense that nothing that we do is as good as it could be, as meaningful as it ought to be, and as fulfilling as it must be.
- Winded by the frantic passing of time, spent by trying to hold on as the world spins by.

The more we try to manipulate our lives to find the things we want, the more we find ourselves weary and worn. The tighter our grasp on the steering wheel, the greater our sense of frazzled lostness becomes. Our attempts to control leave us short of breath and short on life.

I remember that kind of fatigue. For me, it was a Thursday night beginning to a three-night series on The Bible and Archaeology. Thinking that current

information pouring out of Near Eastern archaeological mounds might catch the eye of people seeking
spiritual truth, our church in Milwaukee, Wisconsin,
planned the series for late spring. I spent months
searching the scholarly literature. Piles of books
reflected the broad nature of my research. We talked
about the most relevant material. We narrowed the
field down to the big discoveries. The local camera
shop owner told me how to make slides of the most
exciting material.

The three nights climaxed a week of Vacation
Bible School and other programs. We invited a
campaign group to help. The church ran ads in the
local paper. Our weekly bulletin featured a major
splash on the series.

Finally, Thursday night arrived. The projector
was loaded, the screen was up, the parking lot ready.
I expected a good crowd. I hoped for many visitors. I
planned enough handouts for a hundred people. I
prayed that seekers would see the evidence from the
ancient worlds as reason to believe.

Eight people came. Most of the campaigners
spent the evening out on the town with their host
families. Most of the congregation skipped the event.
All of the unchurched community decided to do
something else. Aside from my family and the
church staff, three people came.

As I stood outside the auditorium caught between
the months of work I had done and the sparseness of
the crowd, weariness filled my soul. Running home
seemed preferable to starting the program. Sleeping
it off offered more solace than sloughing it off. I
faced a kind of exhaustion that I had seldom known.

Exhaustion, not from physical exertion, but from
spiritual emptiness. Weariness, not from lack of
sleep or boring routine, but from living below where

I wanted to live. Sensing triumph, but finding only failure, expecting victory, but experiencing defeat, I was exhausted.

Beaten, but Not Defeated

Weariness is not limited to the modern world. The ancient world depicted on my slides and the peoples discussed in my archaeological lectures were all too familiar with the kind of exhaustion I experienced that night. Yet right in the middle of all that antiquity sits a package of literature that reveals another story. People tired, but never worn out. People weary, but never exhausted. People beaten, but never defeated.

Called the biblical prophets, they wrote in the dreary days of the first millennium B.C. They penned their words from the bottom of wells and from the midst of battle. They spoke from the porches of ancient temples and from the prison cells of famous kings. Many of them would have been delighted to see an audience of eight. Often nobody listened to their prose.

The most amazing thing about these prophets is that their literature survived. No ancient city still stands in the modern world. Gaps dominate the information we've dug out of the ground about defunct civilizations. Archaeology barely pieces together enough of the picture to get a faint outline of life during the prophets' days. Yet in the Bible we have the writing from that period that has not only survived, but continues to inspire.

Jeremiah knew how I felt that Thursday night. He knew about unresponsive congregations and the inattentive public. He knew about the exhaustion of life. One day, a group of young men from the village of Anathoth gathered on the street corner. A couple of them had heard Jeremiah speak. They didn't like a word of it. "Let's chop down the tree while it is still healthy" (Jeremiah 11:19, TEV).

In the twilight of the Jerusalem suburb, the young men conspired to get Jeremiah. More than once, unhappy members of his congregation threatened his head.

Jeremiah had trouble understanding why God allowed it all to happen. "I've placed my cause in your hands. I've proclaimed your message."

I know that feeling. How many days did I spend on that lecture and almost nobody came? In my Thursday night opinion, Jeremiah had every right to be indignant with God. How can he let the bad cause win out over the good one? How can we be expected to go on with so much against us? Nobody can be expected to go on when nothing goes right.

Run with Horses

Nobody expected God's response to Jeremiah: "Jeremiah, if you get tired racing against men, how will you ever run with the horses? Jeremiah, if you can't stand up in the open country, how will you manage to survive in the jungle?" (Jeremiah 12:5, my translation).

Run with horses? God expected Jeremiah to run with horses? We all get tired racing against the clock, not to mention racing against other people. So how can any of us keep up with the horses? I get exhausted trying to live in suburban America; how could any of us survive long in the jungle?

Yet when taken as a whole, the fifty-two chapters of Jeremiah reveal an amazing historical fact: Jeremiah ran with horses. He not only survived, he thrived. He didn't just make it, he topped it out. He didn't live a mediocre life, he lived in the heights.

What did Jeremiah know about horses? How did he find energy to go on? Jeremiah understood the same lesson that his fellow prophet, Isaiah, learned.

Isaiah knew what my Thursday night spot was like. He spoke to ears that couldn't hear. He tried to open the word of God to closed hearts. Isaiah lived among a weary people. People in his time found themselves boxed into their own depressing world. They thought they had no good choices. Every decision was between average and worse. When they tried to walk, they stumbled and fell. When they tried to run, they grew weak. Even the young adults among them became tired and dejected.[1]

Fly with Eagles

Isaiah mounted his pulpit. "This isn't right! Haven't you heard? Don't you know? Where've you been? Have you forgotten?"

Then Isaiah gives one of history's clearest explanations of God. To people who plopped on the sofa after a hard day's work in Jerusalem, to women who wearily fought the crowds at the marketplace, to the men who exhausted the day shearing sheep, Isaiah said: "God never gets tired. Never. Never. He never gets weary. He doesn't ever stumble or fall. He's never been exhausted."

Exhausted eyes looked up. Weary ears anticipated hopeful music. Weary chins raised expectantly toward the pulpit.

"He'll lift you above the problems of life. You'll be so high that you'll feel like an eagle. You'll be able to see things with a different perspective. From those lofty heights, life will take on a sharper hue, a brighter tint. You'll see in ways you never saw before. You'll find an energy in him you never thought was available."

Isaiah's words (40:27-31) promised they would fly with eagles just as Jeremiah had been told to run with horses. Impossible? So it seems to us in our Thursday night weariness. Unlikely? Not at all.

The prophets said two fundamental things. Both issues grew out of their experiences with God. Jeremiah encountered the first one as a young man. He tells the story of meeting God in Jeremiah 1. God offered him a job. When Jeremiah heard the job description, he declined. God reached out and touched Jeremiah's mouth, then his eyes.

The new prophet saw two images. One jumped out in front of him. Jeremiah recognized it as the branch of an almond tree. God told Jeremiah every time he saw the almond tree, he was to remember that the words of God were reliable. Then Jeremiah saw a pot of boiling water tipping over. The scalding water surged toward Jeremiah's homeland. The prophet recognized it as a symbol of the wicked world. To reassure his young charge, God then touched his ears:

> Today I have made you a fortified city, an iron pillar and a bronze wall to stand against the whole land—against the kings of Judah, its officials, its priests and the people of the land (Jeremiah 1:18).

God's message to Jeremiah was clear. I'm in control. My word is reliable. It always has been. It always will be. The world is dangerous. It always has been. It always will be. But I'm in control of my word and the world.

Young Isaiah saw God in the temple. Like Jeremiah he didn't just see God, but he was overwhelmed by the presence and power of God. When God called for volunteers, unlike Jeremiah, Isaiah

raised his hand. Isaiah's moments in the temple
with God convinced him of one fact: God is in control. Nothing touches his sovereignty. Nothing
matches his power. Both prophets spoke out of their
experience of God. Their verse declares the match-
less qualities of a being beyond their own. In him,
they found strength to run with horses. With God in
control, they flew like eagles.

Yet understanding the greatness and centrality of
God was not the only achievement of the biblical
prophets. Their second accomplishment was their
discovery that our energy comes from our sense of
who we are. See how Isaiah got up every morning:

> The Sovereign LORD has given me an instructed
> tongue, to know the word that sustains the
> weary. He wakens me morning by morning,
> wakens my ear to listen like one being taught
> (Isaiah 50:4).

God woke Isaiah every morning with a lesson in
personal esteem. God's word sustains the weary
because it tells us who we are. The Old Testament
prophets' great success was their ability to paint a
picture of an alternative way of life. In the midst of a
dark world, they saw the brightness of God. Their
words described another world. The prophets transformed their firsthand experience of God into words
that defined the best of human nature, that called
for the highest level of human achievement, that
demanded the loftiest effort out of each muscle.

They defined humanity in terms of God. Their
energy for life came not from their own reserves, but
from the resources of God. If our sense of direction
comes from society, we will have no more energy
than society. If our being is defined by the family,
our enthusiasm for life will never rise above the

level our family achieves. If we let education tell us
who we are, we are limited to the energy that our
knowledge provides.

But if our sense of who we are comes from God,
then our energy is boundless, because he is boundless. Our stamina is endless because he is endless.
Our vitality is perpetual because he is perpetual.

If our ideal in life is another person, we will never
rise above that person. If the best we ever hear
about is an Olympic star, if the best we ever strive to
be is patterned after a television talk show host, if
the deepest we ever think is like our college history
professor, if the most we ever stretch is like the first
baseman for our favorite team, we are doomed to
crash, just as all those people will fall.

God's View

But when we think like God, we see the world in
a different way. In the midst of siege, we'll see peace.
In the middle of exile, we'll start talking about
homecoming. On the hill of crucifixion, we'll see
salvation. In the midst of death, we'll see life. When
we think like God, we will soar with eagles, we will
run with horses.

All around us, we're offered definitions of reality
that hardly make it out of the bedroom, views of
culture that center in the wallet, perspectives on
people that reject anything different, and visions of
tomorrow that repeat the worst of today. If our energy source is any lower than heaven, we'll crawl in
the shadow of eagles and walk in the dust of horses.

As long as we try to control our lives, our energy
is limited to whatever we can get from our inner
furnaces. When we strong-arm our work or dictate
our ministries, then our source of power will be

whatever we can scratch together from our own stamina. Trying to stay in control typically uses up whatever self-generated energy we have. Just handing over control to God maximizes our own sources of energy and allows access to his awesome power.

Both Jeremiah and Isaiah learned that there is a source of emotional energy and physical power that transcends our need for sleep, good food, and recreation. As God's power reformed their self-definitions, they found a passion for life, a drive for ministry that no cycle of sleeping, no ideal diet, no vacation spot could supply. I don't know how much energy God can give me. I only know I've never yet used all he offers.

This formula for finding energy didn't end with the prophets of old.

Above the Inner City

I didn't expect to find horses in the inner city, but an afternoon of ministry with an urban minister amazed me with new discoveries. Billy lives in a run-down apartment in one of the most dangerous sections of our city. It's not Billy's place; it belongs to his younger sister, who shares it with her boyfriend. The worn-out sofa reeked of cigarette smoke, the scarred table was decorated with an out-of-place plastic plant. A cockroach near the front door worked its way through the jungle of dirty shag carpet. The only bright spot in the dingy apartment was Billy's smile. When we got out the Easy-to-Read Version of the Bible, Billy beamed even more. We worked our way through three verses of Luke 14 over the next forty-five minutes. The urban minister skillfully applied each teaching to Billy's world.

We heard a gunshot outside the window as we talked. I watched Billy's fright-filled face turn toward

the window and then back to the conversation with
the inner city minister and me. Billy knows all about
gunshots in this neighborhood. It's where he killed a
man. Billy shot him in cold blood. Sirens screamed.
The police pursued, and Billy left in handcuffs. They
sent him to prison where, instead of learning more
street smarts, he heard about God.

Now you ought to hear Billy talk. Life is a clean
sheet of paper. The old marked up, torn, shredded
piece has been tossed aside. Billy feels guilty for
what he did, he's pained by the hurt he's caused his
family, he recoils from the horrors of prison, he
endures the stares from the family of the man he
killed. But Billy's not a defeated man. He spoke with
enthusiasm and pride about the influence of his
Downtown church in the inner city. We laughed
when he talked about how God has reversed the
impossible: an ex-convict leading a holy life in a
spiritual community where he's finally found a home.

I left his home that afternoon amazed. Out of
such a dark world has come a man of light. Out of
prison has come a freed man. Out of a life of crime
has come a testimony to the imagination of God.
Isaiah would have recognized Billy as one of his.
Jeremiah would have smiled. Some say that, because of crime and poverty, Billy won't make it. But
Billy now sees the world from an eagle's point of
view. He runs with the horses.

Traveling in Ukraine

I expected to find exhausted people in the former
Soviet Union. What I didn't expect were eagles. In
early 1991, five Americans traveled to Kiev, Ukraine,
where we ran a couple of ads in the paper indicating
that several preachers would talk about God and the
Bible at the Union Hall on Thursday, Friday, and

Saturday nights. We had no idea what to expect. We visited the 700-seat auditorium during the day, praying that people would come. That night we arrived early, prayed in a side room, and then shortly before 7:00 started for the stage door.

We couldn't get in. A crowd blocked the entrance. When they saw us, they parted like the Red Sea. We walked through the walls of people into the huge auditorium. I'll never forget that moment. Not only was every seat taken, but adults sat on the floor between the front row and the stage, people stood in each aisle seven or eight deep, and eyes peered through each exit as far as we could see.

On the last night, we promised to distribute free Ukrainian Bibles. Then we realized that the four hundred Bibles we brought in our suitcases couldn't satisfy the thirteen hundred people packed into the Union Hall. Rather than create problems, we told the assembly we would mail each one a Bible. After the program, thirty to forty people gathered around me asking questions. Having heard two hours of preaching, they now spent an additional hour trying to get individual attention. One man in the crowd with long, gray hair caught my eye. Dressed in coarse khaki clothes, worn with the years, he tried to catch my attention by waving his left arm. His large hand, filled with cuts, reflected a hard life. Finally he asked his question, "Can I have a Bible?"

I tried to explain we just didn't have enough, but he would get one in the mail. I watched his chin fall and his shoulders sag. Unclear about his response, I asked about his story. He lived north of Kiev in a village called Chernobyl. When the nuclear power plant exploded in 1986, the government took his house and garden. Deprived of his home, he had lived in poverty. Now a group of Americans had promised him a Bible they couldn't deliver.

"Enough! Enough!" he said. Something about the man's response, something about his desire for God moved me. I felt God wanted something good to happen to this new friend. I asked him if he would be willing to wait on me. He agreed.

When the crowd cleared out, the two of us went to a dark corner. I pulled out a Ukrainian New Testament I had hidden in my vest pocket. When I presented it to him, his face broke into a broad smile. He thanked me repeatedly. He told of how helpful this would be in his quest for God.

Just then one of my American friends walked by with his camera. I thought, "Kodak moment." My Ukrainian friend agreed to pose for a picture. At the last moment, it occurred to me that the photo would look more impressive if we were shaking hands. Without thinking, I reached for his right hand.

He pointed to his empty sleeve. I hadn't seen it. In the crush of the crowd, in the midst of the chaos, I had not noticed. He told me he lost his arm in World War II.

I've thought a great deal about that one-armed man. I called my American friend four months later. He looked through twelve rolls of film, but never found the picture of me and my new friend. Each time I return to Ukraine, I scan the crowds for him. I ask the growing number of Christians if they have seen a one-armed man. The answer is always no.

He's a stranger to all the good life that I've always known. He lost his arm. He lost his farm. He lost his health. He almost lost the opportunity to get a copy of the Bible. Yet despite these exhausting circumstances, despite the weariness of living in an atheistic land, even in his extreme poverty, the smile on his face when he opened his new Bible made me realize what it means to fly like an eagle and to run with the horses.

Thinking about my one-armed friend has helped me overcome experiences like my Thursday night discouragement. Despite that example, though, I became disillusioned with our efforts to help the Ukrainians. After the first two years, our attempts seemed to lose their focus. Our message seemed inhibited. Our efforts mediocre. I got weary and discouraged.

During one meeting in Kiev, a group of Memphis doctors met with sixteen people who stood in the radiation snow the day Chernobyl exploded. Dying of rare diseases, they sought not medical care, but some end to the weariness of their souls. They needed something beyond physical healing. They sought a reason for life. They told us they were from Troeschina, a section of the capital city of Kiev where the government resettled Chernobyl victims. We began to pray that God would open a door there.

Soaring in Troeschina

In early 1994, we took a team of Bible teachers to Troeschina. We taught about God in the classes of a public school and then visited with the principal, Alexander Juirko. His school tripled the building's capacity, so they ran three complete sessions each day for kindergarten through eleventh grade. Alexander told us he was known as the "Chernobyl Director." We asked why.

"We have 1,500 children here from Chernobyl. Many of their parents still work at the power plant one hundred miles away. Sometimes the parents are gone for two weeks at a time. Many of these children are ill. Some are bald from radiation poisoning. Some faint in the hallways. A few have thyroid problems.

Many have nightmares, recalling memories from the night the plant exploded. The government funnels all of its food and medical aid through the school."

We asked if they had a medical facility there.

"We have a medical room. However, it is empty. It aches my heart."

We proposed bringing medicines to fill the room. Then we suggested that we come back in the summer to teach the children about God. We waited for Alexander's reply. "I'm an atheist. But I think the children should be taught about God. We've been looking for someone like you to come. If you can return, there will be no end to the work you can do."

I'll never forget sitting in that principal's office. After feeling for months like we were going backwards, after feeling exhausted in every attempt to do something good and right for these people, after facing repeated frustration, I felt like flying like an eagle. I felt like running with the horses.

Jeremiah and Isaiah were right. Who we are depends on God. When we understand that, we find an inexhaustible source of energy that enables us to run with horses and fly with eagles.

Handing over control to God maximizes our own sources of energy and allows access to his awesome power.

Notes

[1]Eugene Peterson, *Run with Horses* (Downers Grove, IL: InterVarsity Press, 1983).

Focusing Your Faith:

1. We know that sleep will relieve physical fatigue. What do you do to remedy mental or spiritual weariness?

2. What encouragement would you offer a friend who has just suffered a "Thursday night discouragement"?

3. If you could see from God's perspective, how would you now view your problems? What is your new vision of your future?

4. Recall a time in your life when you credit God for giving you the energy to run with horses and soar with eagles.

5. What is your response to God's powerful reversal in Billy's, the reformed ex-convict's life? Are you amazed? skeptical? longing for the same reversal?

6. When have you or a friend stopped pursuing a godly dream because of closed doors? How do these stories shape your future outlook?

7. How could the Troeschina story influence your personal efforts to reach out despite discouraging circumstances?

Luke 7:41–8:3

"Two men owed money to a certain moneylender. One owed him five hundred denarii, and the other fifty. Neither of them had the money to pay him back, so he canceled the debts of both. Now which of them will love him more?"

Simon replied, "I suppose the one who had the bigger debt canceled."

"You have judged correctly," Jesus said.

Then he turned toward the woman and said to Simon, "Do you see this woman? I came into your house. You did not give me any water for my feet, but she wet my feet with her tears and wiped them with her hair. You did not give me a kiss, but this woman, from the time I entered, has not stopped kissing my feet. You did not put oil on my head, but she has poured perfume on my feet. Therefore, I tell you, her many sins have been forgiven—for she loved much. But he who has been forgiven little loves little."

Then Jesus said to her, "Your sins are forgiven."

The other guests began to say among themselves, "Who is this who even forgives sins?"

Jesus said to the woman, "Your faith has saved you; go in peace."

After this, Jesus traveled about from one town and village to another, proclaiming the good news of the kingdom of God. The Twelve were with him, and also some women who had been cured of evil spirits and diseases: Mary (called Magdalene) from whom seven demons had come out; Joanna the wife of Cuza, the manager of Herod's household; Susanna; and many others. These women were helping to support them out of their own means.

Chapter 9

Making Jesus My Money Manager

❧

$\mathcal{Y}$ehizaveta seemed tense. It was our fourth
visit to her facility. She always welcomed us with
open arms. On a previous visit, she invited our
medical missions team to the hospital canteen for a
delightful Ukrainian meal, where she tried to teach
us some Russian words, including the name of a
delicious Ukrainian dessert called nalisniki. I
couldn't say it correctly. It kept coming out something like sneaky-sneaky. The English-speaking
crowd thought it was hilarious. The locals doubled
over with laughter. I think the Ukrainian medical
staff still calls me "Sneaky-sneaky" behind my back.
Now those fun times seemed so far away.

Yehizaveta had good reason to be tense. As head
of the 260-bed Children's Hospital in Bela Tserkva,
Ukraine, Yehizaveta led a 760-member staff, including 188 physicians divided into ten departments.
Not only did they serve the fifty thousand children
in the region, but they also trained doctors and
nurses in pediatrics. She juggled that while also
trying to deal with a budget slashed in half in the

post-Communist economic depression in Ukraine. Yet Yehizaveta had never been this tense.

Finally, we sorted out the problem. The city government had just cut the funds she was using to feed the children in the hospital. Not by 50 percent, but by 100 percent. She had no food for the young-sters in her care. It hurt her to see them suffer from hunger when they already faced injury and disease. Knowing Yehizaveta, she was busy working on some way to get food for the hospital.

Nothing could have prepared me for what came next. David, one of the members of our mission team and an elder, took Yehizaveta aside. They talked through the translator in hushed tones. Words like "budget," "food costs," "availability," and "how much" filtered past the confines of their huddle. Then, from my corner of the room, I saw David reach for his wallet. A smile broke out on Yehizaveta's face. A buzz filled the room. The message was clear: the children will eat this week!

Suddenly the room filled with the same lively spirit we had experienced on our previous visits. The problem weighing on Yehizaveta's heart disappeared. Her reaction to David's gift stimulated everyone.

What surprised me was my own reaction. While visions of children happily eating sneaky-sneaky delighted my heart, and while the local missionary and I exchanged our astounded reactions to the gift, I was surprised at feeling shame. I tried to sort out why I felt bad when I should have felt good. God had just worked through one of his servants to bring good news to a whole hospital. Why, when I wanted to celebrate, was I instead climbing out of the dumps? When I should have felt the brightness of joy, why did I feel the dampness of the cloud of guilt? Sure, I was happy for the kids, delighted for Yehizaveta, moved by David's generosity, but the whole affair caused me a painful self-evaluation.

Then I realized that David's gift shed so much light in the room that I saw my own hand locked on my wallet. The brightness enabled me to see the iron grip that kept my money in my pocket, my investments in the bank, my dollars earning interest, while funds from another flowed into nourishment for children. I felt shame because, in light of such generosity, my own stinginess, my own control over money fell far below my own self-expectations.

The afternoon in the Ukrainian hospital reminded me of God's incomplete work in my life. While he had achieved marvelous victories on several fronts, my natural inclinations about money conducted guerrilla warfare with the divine impulse. My friend's gift to the children again exposed the incompleteness of God's work in my life. More significantly, it revealed to me that of all the areas where I sought to maintain control, money was the one I gripped the tightest.

It's Hard to Let Go

God wants control of our lives. He wants to rule our schedules, our families, our wants, our businesses. He wants our time, our focus, our energy. Choosing God's control is never easy. Few of us consistently let him rule all of those areas, but nothing about my own power-hungry spirit troubles me more than my control over money.

With the sweet taste of nalisniki on my tongue, with the joy of Yehizaveta's celebration fresh in my mind, and with my own inability to release control of my money recently exposed by the light of David's gift, I began to wonder why I gripped my money so tightly. Four trouble spots surfaced.

Safety in Secrecy

First, I don't want to tell you how much I make. My tax liability is a secret. I share the intimate details of my personal finances with a select few financial counselors.

Yet when I become too open about money, others seem to back off or offer unusual advice. Once I shared our family budget with a respected Christian friend and financial expert. He told me I was giving too much to the church and suggested I should cut back.

What we give, how much we spend, the size of our debt, the amount of our retirement, are not easily discussed.

Traveling the financial road alone makes it harder to let go. When I'm the only one who knows what I do with my money, I find it easier to justify autopilot. Fearful shadows and deep ditches make me all the more intent on self-steering my journey. Except in rare times when a gift in a foreign hospital casts so much light on my own life, I find that maintaining control of my cash is a way of indirectly controlling all of my life. Money transforms purse strings into a bridle, controlling nearly every other area of life.

Revolving-door Economics

It's hard to think about altering something that's in constant use. Trying to get a handle on letting go of my finances is like trying to paint a sign on a truck while it's moving. It's like trying to comb a four year old's hair while he's running out the door. How can I think about giving up control of my money when a pile of bills screams to be paid? It's revolving-door economics. Since 95 percent of my monthly income goes to pay for bills I've already incurred, deciding how to spend the remaining 5 percent doesn't rank high on my "to do" list.

No Simple Formula

I also have difficulty giving up control of money because I want clear-cut guidelines. I wish the Bible just had financial charts. If I could turn to 1 Finances 12:34 and find my income in one column and the amount I should give in the next, I'd have fewer problems with this control business. If there were just a section buried in 2 Corinthians listing the approved purchases for a Christian at my stage of development, I'd be happier. A formula in one of the parables telling me that I can spend $50 on new kitchen cabinets for every hour I spend doing church work would definitely help my problem.

But the Bible has no such formula. So I struggle.

Conflicting Advice

Finally, giving control of my financial resources to God is difficult because I hear conflicting advice. Christians often hear two different messages about money. One comes from the Health and Wealth Gospel, the other from the Give and Live Gospel. Let me explain.

The Health and Wealth Gospel says that if I obey God, he will bless me with financial security. Trust God, and move to a bigger house. Do what God says, and your next car will have power door locks. God brokers his rewards through economic avenues. Blessings come as bucks.

Yet while the Health and Wealth Gospel works in one neighborhood, it doesn't play out across town. Some obey God and move up. Others follow God and fall down. The Health and Wealth Gospel works better in rich countries, but seldom speaks to Christians in famine-torn lands.

The Give and Live Gospel says that if I turn it all over to God, he will bless me eternally. Become poor, and God will make sure you have a roof in this life and a mansion in the next. Obey God, and he'll keep you propped up until he takes you up. God sends his blessings by providing the basics. His rewards come at the last minute and in just the right amounts to pay the bills.

I've known several people who follow this version. They've made supreme financial sacrifices. When I have a need, I pray and look at my budget. When they have an expense, they pray. They have no budget. If the money doesn't come, they don't do it. I admire them in many ways. Yet I also see another layer of Christian people who support them, who provide their needs. I've searched the teachings of Jesus for some command that we should all become poor but haven't found it.

I end up confused. Not convinced by either of these gospels, I wonder how Jesus would answer my dilemma. With few people to talk to, with no financial timeouts left, with no mathematical formula in Scripture, what should I do? What clues are there that point to another solution? How would Jesus pry the Visa card out of my hand? I found the answer in an unexpected place. Let me tell you how I imagined it occurred.

Traveling with Jesus

Dogs barked. Sheep scattered. Chickens cackled their way to safety. Children shyly followed but kept their distance. Few visitors came to the village. But twenty people came up the narrow path. It took just

seconds for their arrival to reach the ears of the
eighty or so residents of the small Palestinian ham-
let. As the ministry team of Jesus reached the village water well, nearly everybody from the men
working in the fields to the oldest surviving grandmother found their spot in the crowd.

They had heard about Jesus, but it was his first
visit to their village. Perhaps they expected him to
come alone. It's unlikely they expected him to arrive
like this. The better informed villagers picked out
Jesus right away. They had seen him in Capernaum
or eaten his bread by Galilee. The ones who went to
the Nazareth market each Thursday heard the men
talk about him.

A couple of the villagers quickly counted the
number of men—twelve besides Jesus. The story
they heard about his picking a dozen special assis-
tants was true. One for each tribe of Israel. It was
the Jewish thing to do. Rabbis had their students.
Prophets had their followers. Kings had their royal
court. Jesus had his apostles.

The rest of the mission team shocked them.

Women.

Luke 8:1-3 doesn't tell us the exact number. More
than three for sure. Maybe even seven. Thirteen men
traveling with a group of women? As Jesus taught,
the others ministered. Some helped with the children.
A couple drew water for the mission team, thirsty
after the trip up the mountainside. Two apostles
helped the older villagers find comfortable seating.
Jesus talked about the Gospel of the kingdom. He
always talked about the kingdom. It was his mission.
He could do no less.

Afterwards, the mission team mingled with the
crowd, answering questions, serving the people,
finding out the needs, making plans to depart for the

next village, or perhaps laying plans for where to spend the night.

Yet the villagers couldn't get one thing out of their minds. The women. Not just any women. These were wealthy women. Luke tells us they funded the mission team. When Jesus bought bread, when bedrolls needed repair, when wineskins wore out, they paid the bills.

Men and women weren't equal. Jesus shocked the woman next to the Shechem well in Samaria when he spoke to her. Jewish men didn't talk to women in public. Not only did Jesus visit with women in public, he also traveled with them. Not only did they make the ministry circuit, they also supported him!

Why Women?

The villagers are not the only ones amazed. I'm surprised, too. Why did Jesus need the women to support him? Did God send Jesus to earth without any cash? If we peeked at the heavenly budget, would the line item "Earthly Ministry of Jesus" be all zeroes? After all, he was born in a manger, not in a castle. He traveled with saddle bags, not money bags. He came without a wallet filled with cash; he left without a will for his estate.

Yet Jesus had certain financial abilities. Besides being able to walk on water, raise the dead and cure disease, he could do things that could turn a profit, like making wine out of water, turning rocks into bread, and making coins appear in the mouths of fish. If Jesus could have anything he wanted, then why did he depend on others for support? I know he could do it without them, just as I know he could finance his ministries today without me, but he allowed them and me partnership. Why?

I also wonder why it was a group of women that

supported him. Maybe I'm surprised just because I'm
a man. Maybe if I had grown up in another culture I
wouldn't be so surprised. Yet in that culture women
were not equal to men. Why did Jesus only draw
financial support from women?

Women not only supported his ministry, they
played a crucial role. Many people resisted Jesus in
the Gospels, but there's no record of any women
opposing him. When his supporters fled from the foot
of the cross, the only ones who remained to the end
were women. While the male disciples barricaded
themselves in the upper room, the women went to
the grave. The first people to see the resurrected
Jesus were women. When the faithful gathered in
Jerusalem prior to Pentecost, the crowd included
both genders. Why did these women play such a
crucial role in his ministry?

One more thing catches my attention. Why did
the women who supported Jesus travel with him? I
usually don't expect the people who pay for a ministry to be personally involved. I expect the rich to
send Jesus out while they stay home. Surely, people
wealthy enough to give to Jesus wouldn't have time
to travel with Jesus. But the ministry team that
climbed to the mountainside village included a
number of women—wealthy women.

Why were these women so generous? Why did they
give control of their time and money to Jesus? What
made them relax their control? For years I missed the
answer to all these questions. I'd pondered these
verses, amazed as the picture unfolded, but never had
seen the reason. Then one day I saw it! Those traveling with Jesus included "some women who had been
cured of evil spirits and diseases: Mary (called Magdalene) from whom seven demons had come out;
Joanna the wife of Cuza, the manager of Herod's

household; Susanna; and many others" (Luke 8:2, 3).

There it is! We know almost nothing about them. But one thing we know for sure: Jesus healed the women on the ministry team. They remembered life before Jesus. Mary fought evil spirits. Joanna daily fought disease. Susanna remembered few moments without pain. Then they met Jesus.

Suddenly what he had done for them gave them a clear vision of what they had to do for him. Mary couldn't join the ministry team fast enough. Joanna had to be with him. Susanna committed herself to his work. Receiving grace opens the grip on our money.

Amazing Grace

There's nothing about grace in economic textbooks. Financial planners always ask what we make or what we owe, but never what we've been given. There's little grace on Wall Street, even less in marketplaces of depressed economies. But understanding how to give financial control to God has everything to do with grace.

The women who traveled with Jesus illustrated a great spiritual truth. Our spending reveals our soul. We give as we've received. Giving presupposes an understanding of grace.

Grace stands behind all great giving. The more we accept grace, the more we release control of our money. Where your treasure is, that's where we'll find your heart. Where you *will* put your money is where you *have* put your soul.

That helped me understand something that happened to me in high school when I worked for a building contractor named Ralph Smeltzer. All summer long, along with Ralph's two sons, I carried cement blocks, shoveled sand, and dug holes as we put up a church building in Penn Run, Pennsylvania. My relationship with Ralph didn't end at the construction site. After I became a Christian, I ended up spending time at his house. His sons befriended me. Being involved in their home made me feel accepted. Ralph influenced me in some of my most formative days.

One day at church, when I was a senior in high school, Ralph took me aside. He knew our family didn't have much money.

"What do you plan to do with your life?"

"I'm thinking about being a preacher."

"I think that's a great idea."

"Do you plan to go to college?"

"I'd like to, but I don't know if that's possible."

Then Ralph knocked the wind out of me. He pushed me over. Not physically, but spiritually. "Don't worry about the money. If it comes down to money, I'll make sure you get to go to a Christian school."

Like the events at the Ukrainian hospital, my conversation with Ralph confused me. Thrilled at his offer of financial backing, I started to lay definite plans for school. But I also began to wonder about two issues. One was that Ralph said don't worry about the money. But all I did was worry about money because I didn't have any. My parents didn't have enough. All the colleges wanted money. If I didn't have the money, I couldn't go to college. Money meant control, and I didn't have much of either. The lack of money seemed to sink my ship. Then Ralph blew it away like a feather.

I also didn't understand why Ralph wanted to help me. I worked for him that summer, but wasn't the model worker. I preached at church, but wasn't a perfect teenager. I knew his sons, but why help me when he had two boys of his own to put through college? Why would a man not related to me, with no responsibility toward me, who at best benevolently hired a teenager for a special summer project, want to guarantee my college education?

I ended up going to college. Ralph was right. Money wasn't a problem. I'm not sure what all he did behind the scenes, what he prayed, or whom he talked to, but he was right: Money wasn't a problem.

Ralph knew what I had yet to learn. A larger reality loomed beyond the bricks and wood we used in that Penn Run church building. An unseen church building project filled Ralph's heart. He used the money he made from putting up a church building to build up the church. God had changed his life. Now he saw me as an investment in the kingdom just as the women who traveled with Jesus also built up the kingdom. Only an experience with grace makes us see that unseen reality. Only when we see it can we begin to release the grip on our wallets.

Gifts of Grace

Just before Luke tells about Jesus' mission team, he records another episode. At first glance, the two stories seem unrelated, but after self-inspection in the Ukrainian hospital I saw links between them.

While visiting Simon's house, a prostitute approached Jesus to wash his feet. Simon couldn't figure out why Jesus didn't chase her out of the house. Instead of pushing the woman away, Jesus pulled Simon up close and told him the story of two men who owed money to the banker. One had a large debt, the other a small loan. Neither could repay, so the banker cancelled both debts.

Jesus whispered to Simon, "Which of the two men was most grateful?"

Simon got the answer right.

Then Jesus said that the one who is forgiven a small amount, the one who never fully senses the grace he's been given, is usually grateful in small amounts. But people who comprehend the fullness of the gift given to them break out in substantial gratitude. Then Luke follows with a brief reminder that the women who supported his ministry were the ones who had received life-changing gifts of healing. Simon never financed the ministry of Jesus because he never understood the grace Jesus offered him. The women understood that grace. Their gratitude played out in the way they paid the bills.

God often puts two stories side by side, inviting us to see the connection. Luke 7:36-50 about Simon followed by Luke 8:1-3 and the ministry team is not the only time I saw connectedness.

Just after our visit to the Children's Hospital, my friend, Sergey took us to Public School 125. For months he had been begging us to come teach Bible to the students of this kindergarten through eleventh grade school. Since Sergey became a Christian, his life had radically changed. Influencing this school for Christ was just one aspect of that change.

As the son of a school teacher, Sergey played an active role in the parents' organization at PS125. He proudly showed us the school gym, the woodwork shop, and the cafeteria. We taught in the elementary grades and gave gifts to the children.

Later that night, Sergey came to my hotel room. He wanted to give me a gift for coming to his school. I couldn't believe it. I felt I should offer him a present for setting up the wonderful day at PS125. He pulled out a beautiful clear vase of cut glass. Heavy. Obviously expensive. I hesitated to accept it.

Then he told me, "My mother taught school all of

her life. When she retired, the school gave her this vase as a retirement gift. Now, because you have helped us, we want you to have it."

Dozens of thoughts raced through my mind. People don't give up their retirement gifts. This personal memento should stay in the family. Why should this man, who lives in the midst of the economic chaos of newly found freedom, give me a gift?

Then the light from the hospital room gift enlightened me. I saw a connection between the two events. I watched a colleague give because of the grace in his heart. Now Sergey offered me a gift because of the grace God placed in his heart.

I accepted both gifts. The one from my friend, and the one from God.

The lesson taught in Luke 8:1-3 made my experience with Ralph clear to me. It illuminates the hushed conversation in the Ukrainian hospital and the bright smile on Yehizaveta's face. The women who gave to Jesus helped me comprehend Sergey's gift of the vase. It's a lesson I learn repeatedly. People who have received grace pass it on to others. Each time God brings me face to face with the gift of grace, I release my grip a little more.

 Where you will put your money is where you have put your soul.

Focusing Your Faith:

1. David's spontaneous gift to the hospital prompted joy in some and self-evaluation in others. If you had been there with the mission team, what would your response have been?

2. Do you share your financial status with any other Christians, other than your CPA? Why?

3. Why do you suppose Luke recorded the story of Barnabas's public contribution (Acts 4:36, 37) since many Christians seem to believe that giving should be done in secret?

4. Recall a time when someone's gift encouraged you to give more generously.

5. Do you most often follow the Health and Wealth Gospel or the Give and Live Gospel? Why?

6. Read 2 Corinthians 8:1-5. What similarities do you see between the Macedonian churches and the four women on Jesus' ministry team?

7. What motivates your giving most: a specific need; the church budget; feelings of guilt; or spiritual forgiveness and healing?

Luke 6:27-38

But I tell you who hear me: Love your enemies, do good to those who hate you, bless those who curse you, pray for those who mistreat you. If someone strikes you on one cheek, turn to him the other also. If someone takes your cloak, do not stop him from taking your tunic. Give to everyone who asks you, and if anyone takes what belongs to you, do not demand it back. Do to others as you would have them do to you.

If you love those who love you, what credit is that to you? Even "sinners" love those who love them. And if you do good to those who are good to you, what credit is that to you? Even "sinners" do that. And if you lend to those from whom you expect repayment, what credit is that to you? Even "sinners" lend to "sinners," expecting to be repaid in full. But love your enemies, do good to them, and lend to them without expecting to get anything back. Then your reward will be great, and you will be sons of the Most High, because he is kind to the ungrateful and wicked. Be merciful, just as your Father is merciful.

Do not judge, and you will not be judged. Do not condemn, and you will not be condemned. Forgive, and you will be forgiven. Give, and it will be given to you. A good measure, pressed down, shaken together and running over, will be poured into your lap. For with the measure you use, it will be measured to you.

Chapter 10

Broken Bridges

The *New Yorker* ran a cartoon with a picture of a small bridge bearing a sign that said: "Load Limit—8 Tons." A truck crossed the bridge. Painted on the side of the cab were clear letters reading: "Weight—8 Tons." Just when the truck reached the middle of the bridge, a bluebird landed on the highest girder. The bridge gave way, crashed into the river below, taking truck and driver with it, leaving behind a confused bluebird.

Have any bluebirds landed on your bridge? They land on mine all the time, especially my relationship bridges. More than once I felt the strain of that extra weight.

I keep a spiritual journal that records the lumps and bumps along with the harmony and serenity of my life. This year I'm reading back through last year's journal. I turned to a page of some painful memories, some sweet relationships turned sour. As I read my record of painful thoughts, I tried to remember how our friendships had cracked. In retrospect, it seemed as innocent as a baby bluebird landing on the top of a delivery truck, but it broke the bridge that linked us together.

You know the feeling. Broken relationship bridges threaten us at every turn in the road. Do any of these sound familiar?

- My neighbor is in his fifth week of giving me a hard time about the rotten wood in the fence. I'm not sure how much more I can take.
- The junior high health teacher keeps adding questionable material to my son's class. I've got to do something soon.
- I've said all the right words to my friends grieving over a tragic death, but I sense rejection and ineffectiveness.

Maybe other bluebirds bother you. Have any of these overloaded your circuits?

- You had to compete against a friend for the same promotion . . . and now try to remain friends.
- You are working on your marriage, but your spouse seems increasingly unresponsive.
- Even though you've been dating for two months, you're increasingly unsure about the future of that relationship.

Those short sentences reflect long stories. It doesn't take long to remember relationships that have come up short. Each one has some event, some word, some action that, like the bluebird, caused the relationship to crash into the gully below.

Suffering through Relationships

Bill and I loved Pirate baseball. We'd sit down the third-base side, eat hot dogs, and cheer the Bucs. The long drive to the stadium gave us time to talk.

Bill was a special friend in many ways. We met one month when his life was spiraling downward. I sat in on sessions with the lawyer that finally got things worked out. Out of walking that tough road together, we formed a bond. I led Bill to Christ. I watched him grow as a leader in our church. Our families participated in our friendship.

During one of our big family get-togethers, Bill met my cousin Steve. After doing a few things together, problems erupted. One night the bluebird landed. Both lost their tempers, said regrettable words, made impulsive vows. Regret replaced joy. Bitterness filled in for camaraderie. Tension displaced friendship.

I didn't know how to feel. Why was Bill angry with me when his fight had been with Steve? Why was I rejected when Steve was responsible? Why did I have to lose a friend instead of a cousin?

Should I feel guilty for introducing them? Did I somehow undermine their relationship? Nothing made sense. Nothing added up. Nothing helped.

About a month after the bridge fell into the gully, Bill dropped by to pick up a bicycle he had loaned me. We talked politely. We loaded the bike carefully. We avoided the issue consistently. Somehow we knew that in putting the bike on the back of the car, we were burying our relationship. As we stretched the straps, we closed the casket. As we checked for loose ends, we erected the tombstone: Relationship. Born 1969. Died 1971.

Never have I felt so out of control. I wanted Bill to be my friend, yet I let him go. I hated what had happened, but felt powerless to undo it. I regretted the loss of my friend, but everything I did seemed to push him away. Severed. Cut off. Estranged. Guilt-ridden. Confused. Tender.

A Healing Prescription

Like most medicines, the antidote to my crushed soul caused pain and yet promoted healing. The prescription for renewed relationship health comes in Luke 6:27-38. Salve for a wound inflicted by an enemy who tries to bring out the worst in us. A remedy for the person who gives me a hard time. A medication for those who take advantage of us. Stitches for my relationship with Bill.

This passage is filled with imperatives:

- Love your enemies;
- Do good to those who hate you;
- Bless those who say bad things about you;
- Offer the other cheek;
- Be merciful;
- Don't judge;
- Don't condemn;
- Forgive.

Suffering from my severed relationship with Bill, the last thing I wanted to hear was a list of things to do. I don't need anything else to do, I need a way to heal. I'm on the edge, and Jesus wants me to do something else. I'm already living beyond my emotional limits, and Jesus calls for an emotional splurge.

Leave me alone.

But Jesus isn't trying to push me over the edge, he's showing me the whole picture. I understand things much better when there's a picture. Putting together children's toys is always easier when they include one of those explicit diagrams. When I ask for directions, I appreciate the folks who take time to draw me a map.

I've never seen a perfect person. I've not met an

individual who totally reflects the grace of God in
her life. I've not watched a person saved by God deal
with life in exactly the way God wants. So Jesus
paints a picture of that person in Luke 6.

The picture illustrates a grace-filled life. It's not a
list to follow to receive grace. We don't have to live
this way to be saved (what a relief!). This is the way
a saved person is called to live. This is what a graced
life looks like, not how a candidate for conversion
appears.

That takes away the pain. Once I understand
that I'm looking at a picture of what I might be with
God's help, not what I must be by my own power, the
healing prescription can have its full effect.

Three healing actions run through this passage.
None work independently. Each joins with the other
to restore severed relationships, to protect our
sensitivities from the sharp edges of life.

Practice Kindness

The first treatment for broken relationships
comes in four quick doses:

1. Love your enemies;
2. Do good to those who hate you;
3. Bless those who curse you;
4. Pray for those who mistreat you.

The same medicine comes in all four doses: it's
the medicine of kindness. Kindness doesn't come
easy for most of us. Spite pops out more easily than
appreciation. A caustic spirit grows quicker than a
caring spirit. Ugliness often crashes our relationship
bridges into the gully of pain and agony.

Most insurmountable relationship problems can be
solved by kindness. Many of the destructive forces in
society can be routed by mercy. Our greatest antidote

is love. Our most powerful injection is kindness.

A few years ago, the *Catholic Digest* carried the story of Philip Kelly, a Franciscan monk who worked with Puerto Rican migrant workers in New Jersey. They picked tomatoes for Campbell's, vegetables for Bird's Eye, blueberries for everybody else. Most workers hoped to make enough money to buy a house back home.

Migrant worker Walter Jensen worked the fields for forty years. Everybody loved Jensen. At Christmastime, each worker put one day's wages (about five dollars) into a pot for a drawing. The winner got enough money to spend Christmas in Puerto Rico. One Christmas, they asked Kelly to draw the winning name. He reached in the pot, pulled out a handful of names, picked one. Kelly opened the paper and read the name.

The winner: Walter Jensen.

The workers cheered Walter's good luck. As a celebration on Jensen's behalf broke out, Kelly reached back into the pot. He started looking through the slips of paper. Each was written by a different hand, but every slip had the same name: Walter Jensen.

That's kindness. That's the kind of spirit Jesus says heals broken relationships. Yet this treatment works best when accompanied by another procedure.

Forgive

Look at Jesus' prescription:

- Do not judge, and you will not be judged;
- Do not condemn, and you will not be condemned;
- Forgive, and you will be forgiven.

Back during the depression, Jim and Betty received a roomful of wonderful wedding gifts. They left the items at her parents' house while they made their wedding trip to Atlantic City. When they came home, the presents were gone. Betty's mother sold them. Times were tight. She saw an opportunity and took it. The mother and daughter argued. They exchanged accusations.

For the next thirty-three years the two families lived in tension. Betty kept her mother's misdeed at the front of the relationship. Geographically they resided three miles apart. Emotionally they lived in different worlds. The grandchildren never knew their grandmother because of the resentment their mother harbored over the sold wedding gifts. They never made up. And Betty's mother died.

Only one remedy would untangle such a relationship mess. Only one procedure could sort it all out, but neither woman would forgive the other.

I speak with such assurance because I've seen it work. Ron and Shirley meant a great deal to our small congregation until certain rips and tears began to appear in their relationship. Finally, they revealed that they had each been involved in affairs. He slept with his secretary at a motel on the south side of the city. She stole away to a single friend's house during the day. They dropped the task of getting them back together in my lap.

Fortunately, they had built some strong relationships with fellow Christians. Using those links, we built a case for mutual forgiveness. We worked through all the objections: What if? But she. He lied. She went first. He cheated more. Right in front of my face. The list went on.

But one night around the table, they forgave each other. The forgiveness didn't remove the treacherous past, it didn't erase the harsh words or blot out horrible memories of passion shared with another, but it was enough to start rebuilding the family house.

I know what you're thinking. I know because I've thought it, too. Right now you're saying this to yourself: "Naw! No way!"

Forgiveness often ends up a one-way street. The mother will forgive, but not the daughter. The wife offers her hand, but he bites it off. The friend seeks out the other, but he won't answer the phone or return the letters.

I know. I tried kindness with Bill. I tried forgiveness. Neither worked. We remained estranged. The gully was too deep. The bridge was too severely damaged. The chasm could not be filled.

What happens when kindness and forgiveness fail? Jesus offers the final solution.

Let God Be in Control

The third procedure Jesus recommends is not our natural tendency. We usually think like this. Hit the enemy before he hits me. Strike while he's asleep. Get in line first. Arrive early to beat her out. Find the weak spot and take full advantage of it.

Jesus says that's strong-arming life. He says no. Try another approach. Decide what you'd most like the other person to do for you, and do it to her first. Instead of putting yourself number one, put the other fellow number one. Get in line first, and let somebody else in front of you. Strike a good deed for him while he's still asleep.

The healing action Jesus prescribes, the medicine he wants us to take, the surgical procedure he recommends is simple: Hand control over to God.

- Only when I give up control to God can I heal enough to be kind again.

- Only when I surrender the problem to Jesus can I see my way to forgive.
- Only when I let go can I get my life back.
- Only when I recognize my own ineffectiveness can I seek the power of God.

Strong-arming life keeps us from kindness. Riding roughshod on relationships keeps forgiveness corralled out of sight. Trying to control our relationships on our terms leads to lives roaring out of control, burdened with relationship failure, and crashing into the gully, truck and all.

Listen to what I thought. If I can't force this relationship with Bill back together, then chaos will break out. Giving up control leads to anarchy. I have to rule with an iron hand. The more I tried to arrange reconciliation, the more I depended on myself, the further Bill and I split, and the more unhappy my own life became.

Life-changing Rewards

Two things changed my mind. One was Genesis 1. "In the beginning God created the heavens and the earth. Now the earth was formless and empty. . ." (verses 1 and 2). Everything was out of control. Nothing worked. Disorder reigned. Chaos ruled. It's the kind of life I detest. It's the environment I fear. It's the world I resist.

Then Genesis 1 continues. God spoke. The planets lined up. The elements obeyed. The waters stood at attention. What I wanted, God did. God formed the formless. God filled the empty. God created order out of chaos.

It made me realize that if I chose to give control to God, I was giving control to the one who took chaos and created order. Giving up control didn't mean sure formlessness, it meant certain order. God organized the day and night, not me. God brought order out of disorder, not me. God pushed back the chaos, not me.

Maybe it is okay to give God control.

The other text that changed my mind was this one in Luke 6. The three themes of kindness, forgiveness, and giving up control all lead to one final result: Reward.

- Your reward will be great;
- You will be sons of the Most High;
- It will be given to you, good measure, pressed down, shaken together, running over.

Incredible! Practice kindness. Forgive. Let God be in control. Add them up, and I get REWARDED!

What I least expected is what I get. That's the way God works.

Remember the pictures of the young people chopping away pieces of the Berlin Wall and the nightly newscasts about Gorbachev's dismantling of the USSR? In the middle of all our amazement, a friend called, asking me to go with him to Ukraine to help start churches.

That phone call began a ministry to the wonderful people of the ancient city of Kiev. The response to our running of six two-inch ads in the local newspaper amazed us. Well over a thousand Ukrainians sat for two hours listening to each translated word as we talked about God and his wonderful Son.

We dreamed that they would follow Jesus. We envisioned filling the nation with Bibles, planting churches in every city, and restoring the body of Christ among the Ukrainian people. We wanted to take the cause of Christ to fifty-two million people who had survived seventy-two years of atheistic socialism.

A year later, I prepared to take another trip to central Ukraine to pursue those dreams. But instead of the optimism of the earlier trips, I felt pessimistic about the opportunities. Many had been led to Christ. Many of them became personal friends. But now they began to resist us. The ones we had taught raised objections about our efforts. I felt like our relationship bridges were swinging dangerously.

> *The three themes of kindness, forgiveness, and giving up control all lead to one final result: Reward.*

My sense of control told me that I should pursue my goals to the end. My investment was at risk. I needed to get a tighter grip. So I squeezed. I tightened. I prepared for battle. By my own iron-will discipline, I decided that nothing would stop me from my vision of churches all over Ukraine.

Then came the moment. I met with a group of new Christians. We sat on worn benches in an antique classroom. Two years before, the new Christians had been Communists, either willingly or unwillingly. Two years before, they were not permitted to own Bibles or hold religious assemblies. Two years before, they had existed in a world where *church* was a synonym for *museum*. Now they sought to follow Jesus. Then it hit me. At that moment, I realized that the force fighting my mission, the source of the resistance to my dream was . . . a church.

What I thought was a collapse of a relationship bridge was the relationship span God had been building. I was the bluebird about to crash it into the gully.

Once I realized what God had done, I released my control to him and tried to live a life of kindness, seeking their forgiveness for my anguished frustrations.

As I've read last year's spiritual journal, I've been struck at the deep emotions recorded there. Anger at people who upset me. Disappointment when certain things didn't happen. Worry over upcoming events. Frustration at how slowly things moved. Discouragement at relationship problems. Bitterness at unanswered prayer. Confusion about why certain things happened.

But do you want to know my biggest discovery?

I'm amazed at how small most of those things seem in retrospect. I'm stunned at how much emotional energy I spent on issues that lasted only a week. I was struck by how many pages I could write about problems that I now don't even remember. I was astonished at how God worked out such simple solutions to these difficult problems.

When I gave him control, kindness and forgiveness came easier. Even in unresolved relationship problems like the one I have with Bill, it has only been through giving up control to God that I've found any peace at all.

Not everyone has to keep a spiritual journal. But everybody must have spiritual rewards. It starts with one simple step: handing control over to God.

 *Incredible! Practice kindness. Forgive.*
Let God be in control. Add them up,
and I get REWARDED!

Focusing Your Faith:

1. Describe a time when you were relieved someone did not do to you what you would have done to them.

2. How did you feel when you did something extra-ordinarily kind for someone you've been at odds with?

3. Do you think it's fair that God will forgive us according to how we have forgiven others? Why?

4. Name the dominant emotion you feel when someone has been unpredictably kind to you. Why?

5. Read Luke 6:29. Can you recall a time when you or someone else applied this Scripture in a real-life confrontation?

6. If you decided to give God total control over your most intimate relationship, would your response be relief or fear? Why?

7. What was your rationale the last time you felt justifiably angry? Would you use the same rationale after reading this chapter?

Matthew 6:1-13

Be careful not to do your "acts of righteousness" before men, to be seen by them. If you do, you will have no reward from your Father in heaven.

So when you give to the needy, do not announce it with trumpets, as the hypocrites do in the synagogues and on the streets, to be honored by men. I tell you the truth, they have received their reward in full. But when you give to the needy, do not let your left hand know what your right hand is doing, so that your giving may be in secret. Then your Father, who sees what is done in secret, will reward you.

And when you pray, do not be like the hypocrites, for they love to pray standing in the synagogues and on the street corners to be seen by men. I tell you the truth, they have received their reward in full. But when you pray, go into your room, close the door and pray to your Father, who is unseen. Then your Father, who sees what is done in secret, will reward you. And when you pray, do not keep on babbling like pagans, for they think they will be heard because of their many words. Do not be like them, for your Father knows what you need before you ask him.

This, then, is how you should pray:

> *"Our Father in heaven,*
> *hallowed be your name,*
> *your kingdom come,*
> *your will be done*
>   *on earth as it is in heaven.*
> *Give us today our daily bread.*
> *Forgive us our debts,*
>   *as we also have forgiven our debtors.*
> *And lead us not into temptation,*
> *but deliver us from the evil one."*

Chapter 11

Prayer: Confessions of a Controlaholic

∽

Wasted prayers.

Be quiet, mind. Don't even think it. Push it out of consciousness. Get it off the screen. Prayers can't be wasted. It's wrong even to think it.

"Ugly thought, begone!"

But it wouldn't leave. It kept seeping through the walls of my mind, penetrating my awareness. It was like an error message appearing at the bottom of my computer screen. Unwanted. Intrusive. Unwelcome. But present.

I didn't want to think it. I didn't want to say it. I'm uncomfortable even writing it. Wasted prayers? How can any prayer be wasted? When that thought came to my mind, I felt arrogant even thinking such a low thought.

Why wouldn't it leave? Why did it keep intruding? I deleted it. I issued orders to deny it entry. But it kept coming back.

Wasted prayers.

It seemed like the only answer. The prayer concerned a godly matter. The prayer came from an honest heart. Repeated petitions, anguished requests, prayed on the knees, issued from the inner soul—everything seemed to be in place, but no answer came at all. Nothing. Things got worse. In fact, everything collapsed.

The thought of wasted prayers penetrates more minds than just mine. Prayers scream from the emergency room hallway, petitions arise from the middle of a domestic quarrel, anguished entreaties unfold when the loved one is five hours late and nowhere to be found. The situations that prompted my "wasted prayer" message fell far short of a major life crisis. It was a common struggle out of daily life that made me reevaluate prayer.

Lessons Lost

On two different days I prayed wasted prayers. One Tuesday I was working on a sermon on Luke 5:33-39. It's the passage where some local religious officials raise the issue of Jesus' piety. They made an unfavorable comparison between how Jesus and his disciples went to parties while John used the same moments to fast and pray with his associates. Jesus responded with the business about not using new cloth to patch holes in old clothes and about not putting new wine in old wineskins.

I had been preaching through the Book of Luke. We preachers love to do sermons in series because working through a biblical book comes easier than learning about a new text or topic each week. As I worked my way through Luke, each lesson gave me new understanding of the flow of the book. The careful unfolding of ideas accumulated in my mind. When I opened Luke 5 that morning, I felt at home; it was familiar territory. I had plowed this field before.

Prayer for My Plan

While mapping out future sermons on Luke several months before, I had jotted down some notes from this passage about our purpose in life. People in the business world are caught up in defining their mission and goals. From _Newsweek_ to the local corporate scene, I'd heard a great deal about being proactive, about identifying purpose, and about accomplishing our mission. God calls us to do the same with our lives. Speaking from this text about our purpose offered something relevant.

Since I knew several months beforehand that a sermon on purpose was waiting offstage, I had started collecting stories on the topic. As I looked through my collection that Tuesday morning, I had some good ones. A real attention getter for the opener and a motivational illustration to wrap it up.

Tuesday morning brought it all together. I had familiar text. I had a cutting-edge topic. I had some good illustrations.

Ready.

Set.

Stop.

I read the text. It didn't say anything to me about purpose. Reread. Nothing about goals. Read again. Wrong topic. Read again. Empty. I thought, "Maybe I need to get the bigger context." I started at Luke 3 and read the next six chapters. The text sang with points to make, but none related to purpose.

Then I prayed. "God, help me to see the link between patches and wineskins, and our purpose in life. Give me creativity. Give me wisdom. Give me imagination. Give me understanding. Help me to see how this all ties together."

Confidently, I got up off my knees, returned to the

keyboard, opened the text, and with great expectation reread it. Fingers stood ready to charge across the keyboard as the relationship between patches and purpose became clear. Illustrations stood at attention on both sides of my open Bible waiting to be used in God's service. Copies of three versions of the Bible opened themselves to provide just the right angle from which to see the connection. A powerful Bible computer program waited to be toggled onto the screen to flood me with instant word study material or cross references. The relevant material could be transferred to my sermon text just by pressing three keys. With my army in place I went back to the passage. Rather than reading the text so quickly, I read at a crawl, pondering each word and comparing versions.

"John trains his disciples better than you do, Jesus."

"Why put new patches on old garments?"

"Don't you see the problem with putting new wine in seasoned containers?"

I didn't see any connection. No link between our purpose in life and the text. Thinking I missed something, I read it again. No link. I read it again. No connection.

Frustrated, I pulled out some commentaries. Wondering what I was overlooking about this passage, I got advice from authorities—Geldenhuys, Danker, Evans, Craddock, Wiersbe, Tiede. Sure that one of them would help me find that missing angle, I turned from the screen to ponder their texts.

Nothing. Not one of them mentioned the obvious connection that this text had with our purpose in life.

Driven to Prayer

Then I realized that God was driving me to prayer.

Smiling at my clever observation, I returned to my prayer closet (actually it's just the black chair at the other end of my study room). I did my ACTS prayer. A—Adoration. I honestly and openly gave God praise. C—Confession. I thought through my weaknesses and miscues, laying them out on the prayer table. T—Thanksgiving. Glancing around the corners of my life, I saw many things to be grateful for and duly mentioned them to God. Finally, I got down to business: S—Supplication.

"God, the sermon isn't going well. I've spent time in the text. You know how many times I've read it. Luke and I are old friends. I've been living inside his mind for six months now. And it's not just Luke that I've been thinking with. I've brought this matter to you before in prayer. Help me see the connection. I have many things to do today. This sermon really needs to be in shape before 5:00. Help me break out of this stalemate. Help me see what needs to be said from this text. Help me relate this to the lives of the people who need some purpose to fulfill."

I thought it was a good prayer. Triumphantly, I returned to the text. Before reading, I decided to go through some of the materials about our purpose in life. Thinking that if I had the questions that bothered people at the front of my mind, I could seek God's response to them as I read the text. Fully loaded, I returned to Luke, confident in finding God's answer to our inability to keep a focus in life. Again I read prayerfully, carefully, slowly, absorbing each new direction, each point, each issue. As I read, I began to understand what Jesus was doing. His statements generated fresh thoughts in my mind. Soon my fingers danced over the keyboard as letters marched across the screen, like rows of soldiers pushing the barriers of ignorance and confusion into retreat. The richness of the text flowed from Luke's words into my thoughts into storage bytes on my IBM. Lines flowed onto the screen at a feverish pace.

Unanswered Prayers

The eruption of thoughts finally slowed to a stop. I reread my notes. I worked my way through the material on the screen, correcting minor errors, and making helpful explanations. Then it hit me.

What I had written had nothing to do with our goals in life. How could I preach a sermon on purpose if the text kept taking me in another direction? A deep sense of frustration set in. Confused, doubtful, and perplexed, I pushed back my chair to consider what to do.

Give up the relevance of the purpose issue?

Find another text?

Take a break?

Find another job?

Pray?

There it was. Prayer will solve every problem. Nothing is impossible for God, not even this lack of connection between this stubborn text and the cutting-edge theme of purpose in life. I just haven't seen it. I need to ask him to open my eyes.

This ritual went on all day. Text. Screen. Prayer. Text. Commentary. Screen. Prayer. Six hours of wrestling. Nearly a full day of pondering.

I left the study room exhausted. I was discouraged not only because I didn't have a sermon written, but because God had not answered my prayers. I couldn't understand why God wouldn't help me.

That's when it started to pop into my mind. Wasted prayer. What other answer could there be? What else could I conclude?

After supper, Sally and I took our nightly walk.

When she asked about my day, I tried to explain my predicament. How could I give birth to a sermon that didn't want to be born? What had gone wrong? What did I need to do? I explained how everything seemed so perfect that morning only to seem wasted six hours later. I didn't mention the wasted prayer to her.

That's when it started to
pop into my mind. Wasted prayer.
What other answer could there be?

The next morning, I prayed for help, changed texts, surfaced another topic, and turned out a set of sermon notes in four hours. I set the notes on Luke 5:33-39 aside, awaiting some new insight. The notes remain untouched, like a monument to a lost battle, like a memorial to the day God refused to answer my prayer. I've not preached on Luke 5:33-39. What I couldn't set aside was the wasted prayer from my wasted day. What could have gone wrong? What was God trying to teach me?

Two weeks later, I pulled out some notes on a text in Ecclesiastes 2. My notes said that we've always heard that everybody has the same amount of time, but not the same amount of money. The Ecclesiastes passage challenged that truism by suggesting that rich people had less time than poor folks because they spent so much time managing their money. I had titled the sermon "Wallet and Watch." Attached to these notes were a couple of promising clippings and stories. Everything seemed set for a grand day of sermon writing. I asked God to direct me as I studied. I plowed into the text.

The next six hours repeated the frustrations and

confusion of the previous sermon writing day. The second time was more discouraging. Wasting one day a month on unproductive sermon writing took the wind out of my sails. Squandering two days in one month left me without a sail at all.

Then it started again. Wasted prayer.

For several weeks, whenever I thought of those two wasted days, that unwelcome thought penetrated my defenses. Down the drain. Nothing accomplished. Nothing learned. Wasted prayer.

Lessons Gained

All that changed when I read Matthew 6. Actually, I was attending a retreat where one of the other participants read the section about prayer. When I heard it read, God suddenly answered the prayers that I had been praying during those two wasted days. How could I have missed it? Why did I ever think it was wasted prayer? In a moment, it all became clear. The prayer from those two wasted days had not been wasted at all. The insight I gained in that one moment of reading represented a substantial gain from my two-day investment. Let me tell you exactly what happened.

Reading the Sermon on the Mount had always been a mountain-top experience for me. I'd preached the sermon twice. I had fond memories of wrestling with each text. Jesus opens the sixth chapter with overlapping thoughts. He presents three thoughts about not practicing our faith on the stage: (1) don't practice compassion to get applause; (2) don't put checks in the collection plate to develop a good reputation; and (3) don't pray for a human audience, but for a divine listener.

The last point becomes the first of three points on

prayer: (1) prayer and the hypocrites; (2) prayer and the pagans; and (3) prayer and Jesus.

Don't Babble

The second point on prayer always confused me. I'd never really understood what Jesus meant by these words:

> And when you pray, do not keep on babbling like pagans, for they think they will be heard because of their many words. Do not be like them, for your Father knows what you need before you ask him (Matthew 6:7, 8).

What did he mean by "babbling like pagans," or, as the New Revised Standard Version translates it, "heap up empty phrases"? What did Jesus imply when he warned about praying "many words"? Sometimes it's helpful to find out what he didn't mean. That's where I started.

Does it mean not to repeat items in prayer? No, Jesus himself often restated the same thoughts. In Gethsemane, he used the same prayer three times. Prayer Psalms like 136 use a repeated refrain. God accepts repetition in prayer.

Does it mean not to pray long prayers? No, Jesus often prayed all night. His petition in Gethsemane went well over an hour. The prayers recorded in 1 Kings 8, Ezra 9, and John 17 seem lengthy to me. Even the encouragement to "pray without ceasing" urges us to believe that God accepts long prayers.

Does it mean not to pray about minor things? Does Jesus warn us about raising petty concerns in prayer? No, Jesus often dealt with problems that bothered only one person. Paul prayed for his thorn in the flesh which never made headlines in the first century. The cryptic advice in Philippians 4:6 is summarized by, "Don't worry, but pray." God anxiously awaits all our requests.

Does it mean not to pray in order to impress others? The first half dozen verses in Matthew 6 make that point. It seems unlikely that "babbling like pagans" referred to praying on the stage. Prayers shouldn't be a theatrical production, but that's not the point here.

What does it mean to "babble like pagans"? How should we understand not praying "many words"?

Don't Pray with Answers

Two other texts helped me uncover his meaning. Paul prays in Ephesians 1:15-23 not that God would give his friends things they do not have, but that God would reveal to them what is already theirs. He prays that the eyes of their heart would be enlightened.

The prayer text in Philippians 4:4-7 reminds us that when we pray, God responds by giving us a peace that exceeds all human understanding. Prayer seeks understanding from God.

Both passages echo the same thought. We pray to *get* understanding, not because we *have* understanding. We pray to get insights and answers, not because we have insights and answers.

That's Jesus' point in the preamble to the Lord's Prayer. The pagans came thinking that they had all the answers and that they needed to let God know what was on their mind. Jesus saw a problem. Human answers are merely "babbling" to an all-knowing God. Earthly solutions become only "empty words" to the mind of God. The pagans used prayer to manipulate God, offering programs for his approval, formulas for his inspection, recommendations for his hearing, and procedures for him to institute.

Prayer for Giving Up Control

Instead, Jesus urges, pray this prayer of giving up control:

> Our Father in heaven,
> hallowed be your name,
> your kingdom come,
> your will be done on earth as it is in heaven.
> Give us today our daily bread.
> Forgive us our debts, as we also have forgiven
>   our debtors.
> And lead us not into temptation, but deliver us
>   from the evil one.
> For yours is the kingdom and the power and the
>   glory forever. Amen (Matthew 6:9-13).

It's a prayer about who's in control. It's a confession of a controlaholic. It's about giving up control.

It's a prayer about who's in control.
It's a confession of a controlaholic.

Each phrase has something to do with control.

Our Father in heaven.

The prayer begins by acknowledging a higher power. I am not king of the mountain, ruler of the band, or king of the road. But in heaven, above and beyond, lives God who is my father.

Hallowed be your name.

Scholars call this an indirect imperative.[1] It means that we're not the ones who make God's name holy, and that we're not telling God to keep his name holy, but we're acknowledging his ability to keep his name sacred. To say "hallowed be your name" is to admit our lack of control.

Your kingdom come, your will be done, on earth as it is in heaven.

With this line, Jesus gives us the words to confess our lack of control. Lead the world, God; I recognize that I'm not in control. You're in charge. What you want is what I want.

Bread, forgiveness, temptation.

Sometimes called the "we petitions,"[2] these requests help us to see our role in life. We seek what we admit we can't do on our own: securing three meals a day; finding release from our mistakes; seeking strength to resist evil. From our stomachs to our relationships, from our friends to our spirits, we need the assistance of our Father.

For yours is the kingdom and the power and the glory forever.

In some late manuscripts, the prayer ends with a shout.

You're in control! The kingdom!

You're in control! The power!

You're in control! The glory!

That's the message I heard at the retreat center when the man in the corner of the room read the Lord's Prayer. Suddenly, the internal battle I waged against the intruding thoughts of wasted prayer ended. I saw that my prayers on those two days had been pagan prayers for a Christian purpose. They were prayers of control, prayers of domination. I wanted to manage, oversee, and supervise. I didn't seek answers, I was dictating solutions. I wasn't petitioning for understanding, I was commanding God's performance. I wasn't looking for the eyes of my heart to be enlightened, I was seeking to en-lighten the eyes of God to the solutions I already saw. I babbled. I prayed many words.

That's why Jesus tells us, "Pray like he's your

father." Don't approach him as the manager of the apartment building where you live. Don't treat him like he's the service manager of the auto dealership. Don't think of him as a client at your office. Don't see him as the police officer who has pulled you over.

Come to him as your father.

The Lord's Prayer enlightened my whole life. My wasted days turned a profit. Now I had room for God in my life.

The Emptying Prayer

An old Jewish folk story tells of man who complained to his rabbi that his house was too small. The rabbi asked, "Do you have a goat?" The man seemed puzzled by the response but indicated he did own a goat. The rabbi told him to bring the goat into his house. After a week of living with the goat, the man returned to the rabbi with the same complaint, "My house is too small." The rabbi asked about chickens. "Do you have any chickens?" He did. The rabbi instructed him to move them in with the goat. Over the next week, at the rabbi's direction, the whole barnyard moved into the house. Finally, the man burst into the rabbi's house shouting, "I am suffocating in my own home. Help me!" The rabbi told him to move all the animals back to the barn.

The next time the man saw the rabbi, he told him he never realized how spacious his house really was.

Once I moved out of the way, I recognized the spaciousness of prayer. Once I moved my agenda out into the hall, carried my formulas to the closet, put my snappy answers in the next room, I discovered that God created more space than I could imagine.

If I've uncovered an essential element toward giving up control of my life to God, it may be this one: the emptying prayer. Jesus gives us the example.

Rather than babble, we acknowledge. Rather than empty words, we empty our hands. Rather than going on and on, we wait on him. Not that the Lord's Prayer becomes a ritual that removes our control, but it serves as an example of the kind of words that can pry our fingers off the controls of life.

> *Rather than babble, we acknowledge. Rather than empty words, we empty our hands. Rather than going on and on, we wait on him.*

My month-long experience with prayer made me realize that, when it comes to prayer, I'm only in kindergarten. I can have the ability to quote a verse from every one of the Bible's sixty-six books and still be a novice at prayer. I can read the text in the original languages and still be learning the language of prayer.

Nothing made me realize that more than my wife's experience in prayer. In the fall of 1990, Sally began to pray that God would help her lead somebody to Christ. She had no prospects. She began to pray for some open hearts and open doors. She shared these excerpts from her prayer journal:

August 21, 1990: I pray for an open door. A door to help reach another person. A woman who has the time and desire to learn more about you. I want to be your servant in this way.

September 6, 1990: I really want to study the Bible with somebody, Lord. Please show me the right person. Lead me to some soul today.

October 14, 1990: Help my purpose to be to bring you glory and to bring others to you. I continue to ask that I can share the Word with someone soon.

November 19, 1990: I want so much to be involved in studying the Word with someone. But it seems that the time isn't right. What are your plans for me, Father? Whom do you want me to share with? Open my eyes so I can see.

December 22, 1990: I continue to ask that I can find somebody open to study with. I pray that the opportunities that come my way will be opportunities sent by you.

In January, our friend Clare invited a woman named Donna to church. Clare and Donna worked at the Memphis Public Library. After Sally met Donna at church, she invited her to lunch at our house. The conversation turned toward God. Sally asked if she wanted to know more about God. Donna seemed eager. The two studied for six weeks. Donna accepted Christ as her Savior in February.

A couple of weeks after her baptism, Donna sent Sally a letter in the mail. She wrote, "I had been praying for a friend who would accept my level of spiritual understanding and encourage me to move beyond it to a higher and deeper relationship with the Lord. I know God arranged it all, for you and me to come together. I praise him for providing an answer to my prayer."

I saw in Sally what I had failed to do myself. To pray the emptying prayer, seeking God to fill my life. Instead, I approached God already full and couldn't understand why my prayers seemed so wasted.

Can prayer be wasted? Yes. Try babbling like I did. Try filling prayer time with empty words. You will find some wasted prayers.

Unless God does for you what he did for me. Through my babbling and empty words, he helped me see the emptying prayer.

Never have I been so full.

We pray to get insights and answers, not because we have insights and answers.

Notes

[1]Douglas R. A. Hare, *Matthew* (Interpretation; Louisville: John Know, 1993), 67.

[2]Ibid, 68.

Focusing Your Faith:

1. Do you agree or disagree that there is such a thing as "wasted prayers"? Why do you feel this way?

2. How have you responded to a seemingly unanswered prayer?

3. Do you devote more of your prayer time begging God to grant your predetermined answers, or petitioning him to grant you a fuller understanding of his will for your life's concerns?

4. In what ways has God communicated his answers to your prayers?

5. Read the Lord's Prayer. What part of this prayer is the most meaningful to you today?

6. Do you know anyone who keeps a prayer journal? How has it been helpful to them?

7. What difficulties have you discovered in releasing control in your prayer life?

2 Corinthians 4:6–5:4

For God, who said, "Let light shine out of darkness," made his light shine in our hearts to give us the light of the knowledge of the glory of God in the face of Christ.

But we have this treasure in jars of clay to show that this all-surpassing power is from God and not from us.

We are hard pressed on every side, but not crushed; perplexed, but not in despair; persecuted, but not abandoned; struck down, but not destroyed. We always carry around in our body the death of Jesus, so that the life of Jesus may also be revealed in our body. For we who are alive are always being given over to death for Jesus' sake, so that his life may be revealed in our mortal body. So then, death is at work in us, but life is at work in you.

It is written: "I believed; therefore I have spoken." With that same spirit of faith we also believe and therefore speak, because we know that the one who raised the Lord Jesus from the dead will also raise us with Jesus and present us with you in his presence. All this is for your benefit, so that the grace that is reaching more and more people may cause thanksgiving to overflow to the glory of God.

Therefore we do not lose heart. Though outwardly we are wasting away, yet inwardly we are being renewed day by day. For our light and momentary troubles are achieving for us an eternal glory that far outweighs them all. So we fix our eyes not on what is seen, but on what is unseen. For what is seen is temporary, but what is unseen is eternal.

Now we know that if the earthly tent we live in is destroyed, we have a building from God, an eternal house in heaven, not built by human hands. Meanwhile we groan, longing to be clothed with our heavenly dwelling, because when we are clothed, we will not be found naked. For while we are in this tent, we groan and are burdened, because we do not wish to be unclothed but to be clothed with our heavenly dwelling, so that what is mortal may be swallowed up by life.

Chapter 12

Glimpses
of Glory

∽

When my sisters and I came home from
church camp, my parents had an announcement:

"We're moving."

"Moving?"

"We're selling the house."

"Selling the house?" How could we sell the house?
For the six of us kids, it was home. Not just a home,
but an experience, a cause, a family project.

When my parents and I moved into the simple
house on Gates Avenue, it had two bedrooms, one
bathroom, and a garage. Over the next dozen years,
my mother had five more children. Dad added two
wings onto the house. We ended up with a five-
bedroom, two-bathroom split level, with room for
two cars in the garage.

Transforming that simple dwelling into a house
big enough for our growing clan became the family
cause. I spent my entire childhood in a house under
construction. We built gables and sanded cupboards.
We dug holes for sewer pipes and installed closets in
the corners of each bedroom. Nothing ever seemed

finished. Everywhere there was evidence that our place was "in process." Stacks of stored bricks land-scaped our front yard instead of shrubbery. A canvas curtain covered the opening to my bedroom instead of a door. Three different colors of shingles decorated our roof. Black Celotex insulation board covered the outside walls. A path led to the front door instead of a sidewalk. Stud walls begged to be covered with paneling. And an eight-inch I-beam stuck out of the side of the house waiting for the addition.

For fifteen years, my father came home from the factory to work all evening on the house. While other families spent the weekend at the lake, traveled in the summer, or gathered with the relatives on holidays, we made rafters in the basement or built kitchen cabinets from scrap lumber or installed our own carpet. We laid our own bricks. We mixed our own cement.

Then that summer, while my sisters and I were at camp, my father gave up. He sold our house.

Growing Disappointment

It was my first real experience with futility. How could we work all my life on a house, bring it right to the edge of completion, put our heart and soul into its walls and floors, and then just sell it? Getting that house in shape gave our family focus. It kept us together. As we lovingly expanded it, the house made room for our growing numbers. To give it away seemed to rip apart the structure of who we were.

It was not my last experience with futility. Two summers ago, I spent every free moment fixing our rain gutters to keep out the leaves. (My father's fix-it-up genes got transferred to me.) After dozens of trips up and down the extension ladder, after getting the best gutter guards, after fixing each guard in place with aluminum rivets, I expected the best results. The next time it rained, the gutters still overflowed because of the leaves.

Last winter our cars took turns visiting the local mechanic. One needed a thermostat. After satisfying it, the other needed a valve job. That done, the first one wanted a water pump, then transmission repair. We supported the mechanic's family for six weeks that winter.

Futility strikes. Disappointment sets in. We lose hope. We verge on giving up. We finish one term paper, only to have another teacher assign a longer one. After wrapping up six weeks' work on the Dallas deal in the morning, we start on the contract with the Boston firm in the afternoon. It takes all morning to clean the bathrooms. Three days later, we reach again for Mr. Clean. The boss calls us in on our first Saturday off in a month. The engine warning light comes on as we head for the beach. The roof still leaks.

Problems with the gutters give way to problems with our adult children. Mechanical difficulties with our second car fail to compare with the malignancy in our spouse's body. Our job doesn't satisfy our lifelong goals. The list of things we can't do any more gets longer than the list of things we still want to do. Our retirement income falls below expectations. Fears of not being able to renew our license or losing our independence mount with each birthday.

No Limitations

The disappointments of life are not limited to those of us who have so much trouble letting God be in charge. Life is full of futility, but when God is reigning in our lives, he turns our life's futility into glory because of Jesus' sacrifice.

Nothing reminds me more of life's disappointment than the bald heads at Sunday morning services. The Matthew House, behind our church's educational wing, offers free accommodations to families who must bring their children to the local medical center for treatment. Rare forms of cancer, obscure life-threatening paralysis, or fast-growing tumors infect their bodies. Moved by their hardships, our spiritual community provides a temporary home for the family ripped from its foundation, threatened by the unknown, and torn apart by a schedule built around radiation treatments and meetings with physicians. Sometimes, during a brief lull in the battle, the youngsters join us on Sunday mornings.

Our teenagers dress up like clowns, roam the wards of the largest children's hospital, pass out balloons, wear painted-on smiles, and spread a message of hope and cheer. Families at church do laundry or fill needs.

But the bald heads speak louder than the painted-on smiles. The constant change of occupants at the Matthew House reminds us all of the constant war with disease.

The fight with disease rips out the family's control. Naive little kids, just like the ones Jesus put on his knee to illustrate humility, pass through the Matthew House with regularity. Children, with no dictatorial control over life and their futures, dangle helplessly at the edge of existence.

Paul's Cry

Each bald head I see in the crowd reminds me of Paul's lament in 2 Corinthians 4–5. His cry of anguish comes in the midst of a seven-chapter-long defense of his work. He talks about control and hardship. He outlines how circumstances forced his ministry team to "not rely on ourselves but on God" (2 Corinthians 1:9). Giving up control is never easy. For Paul, it took being "under pressure, far beyond our ability to endure" (1:8) to force him to give God control. As God increasingly ruled his life, he explained that together "we are therefore Christ's ambassadors" (5:20) which gives our lives focus and meaning. He defends his past behavior with the Corinthian people, reminding them that through the pain God "always leads us in triumphal procession in Christ" (2:14).

Despite being God's man, even in the midst of a God-centered ministry, right in the middle of righteous living, Paul experienced something besides love, joy, and peace. Pain plagued his life.

Being God's man did not end his sense of incompleteness. Working in a God-centered ministry did not remove frustration. Righteous living involved futility. Listen to his lament in 2 Corinthians 4:8, 9: "We are hard pressed on every side, but not crushed; perplexed, but not in despair; persecuted, but not abandoned; struck down, but not destroyed."

Futility vs. Promise

With each statement of hardship comes a word of hope. Hope outweighs futility. Faith outdistances frustration. Paul used three metaphors to describe the tension, three images to capture the dominance of promise over futility:

1. Clay pots versus heavenly vessels.

   But we have this treasure in jars of clay to show that this all-surpassing power is from God and not from us (2 Corinthians 4:7).

We live in a clay flower pot. Our fragility opens us to
futility. Now we crack, break, and leak. In contrast,
we anticipate heavenly vessels which escape futility.
2. Earthly tents versus heavenly houses.

> Now we know that if the earthly tent we live in is
> destroyed, we have a building from God, an
> eternal house in heaven, not built by human
> hands (2 Corinthians 5:1).

We live in Colemanlike tents. They rot, mold, and
leak. But we expect a heavenly house which is not
constantly under construction, has no mortgage, and
never leaks. Futility and faith walk hand in hand.
3. Nakedness versus heavenly clothes.

> Meanwhile we groan, longing to be clothed with
> our heavenly dwelling, because when we are
> clothed, we will not be found naked. For while we
> are in this tent, we groan and are burdened,
> because we do not wish to be unclothed but to be
> clothed with our heavenly dwelling, so that what
> is mortal may be swallowed up by life (2 Corin-
> thians 5:2-4).

Our wardrobes here leave us naked, giving little
protection from rain and cold, offering slight shelter
from bullets or knives, and providing no safety from
bacteria or virus. But future wardrobes will hold
marvelous garments that will protect us from down-
pours, danger, and disease.

Paul's metaphors remind us about the futility of
not having control of our own lives. Living in a house
under construction. Painful arthritis. Piles of unpaid
bills. Cars that won't start. Children who won't be-
have. Broken pots. Leaky tents. Worn out clothes.

Life is filled with adversity. When we try to control
it, we are back to the beginning of this book. We can't

control our lives. We must let God be in control. But
Paul reminds us that even with God in control, even if
you are a chosen apostle of God who has given up
control to God in mammoth ways, the trials do not
disappear. Even when all is in the hands of God, we
continue to experience the hardships of life.

Hope

Yet we are not left there. We have a way of facing
even that struggle. It comes under the title of hope.
Unless we give up our sense of futility itself, until we
deposit ourselves completely in the container of
hope, only when we look into the future do we have
the equipment to deal completely with the struggle
against futility. That's the theme of what Paul tells
us next.

Against the futility of life, in the midst of constant change, in the face of incompleteness, God
offers concrete certainties. We're not just told to
come back later, but we are given some things to
take in the meantime. In the midst of his lament
about life's mortality, he offers a present antidote to
our ailments. In 2 Corinthians 4:14, he offers three
certainties.

1. God has raised Jesus from the dead.

Before the weekend was over, God raised him up.
Before Sunday dinner, God positioned himself to
offer worldwide forgiveness. In three days, God had
revolutionized world theology.

Resurrection wreaks havoc with futility. Jesus'
resurrection let light into a dark world. Resurrection
gave hope to people like us and to folks like Paul.
That's the reason Paul could repeatedly add "but
not" to his laments.

• Hard pressed, *but not* crushed;

- Perplexed, *but not* in despair;
- Persecuted, *but not* abandoned;
- Struck down, *but not* destroyed.

Paul saw that the reason he lived a "but not" life was because of the resurrection.

- Tortured on the cross, *but not* defeated;
- Loaded with sins, *but not* ruined;
- Mocked for perfection, *but not* disgraced;
- Buried in a tomb, *but not* forgotten.

The resurrection empowers our own victory over futility, guaranteeing that mortality doesn't win, generating hope in our souls, positioning us to win the race of life. But the certainties that defeat futility don't end there.

2. *God who raised Jesus from the dead will raise us from the dead.*

Life doesn't end at the Matthew House. Existence doesn't cease in ICU. Memorial Park is not our final address. Resurrection affirms that life goes on. God's hand reaches out of heaven through the sealed vaults, past the granite tombstones, through the concrete walls to take us home.

God writes the final chapter on futility. Nothing we do, inside or outside of Christ, lets us escape. We can't control adversity. We can't give up enough control in order to control suffering. But God promises to pen the closing words. God, not Congress, makes the rules about how the world will end. TV cameras will not be there to cover God's final acts. Hollywood will not make a sequel to the final resurrection.

Nothing flattens futility like the promise of resurrection, unless it's the concluding assurance that comes to Christian people.

3. *God will bring us into his presence.*

The final certainty is a trip to God's house, to enter his living room, to join him on his couch, to sit at his dining room table. Revelation 19:9 reminds us we'll be invited to the marriage supper of the Lamb. Revelation 22:4 tells us we'll see his face. Zephaniah 1:7 calls us to the feast on the day of the Lord.

Nothing ends futility like the reminder about eternal life. Nothing provides a context for the disappointments of this life quite like the banquet table of God. No disillusionment lasts long when we smell the dinner cooking for us at God's house.

Scripture offers a graphic description of what happens to the futility of life. Three times the Bible speaks about futility being "swallowed up." Not only do we get a new vessel to live in, a superior house, and better clothes to put on, but everything old and bad gets swallowed up. Using table imagery, Scripture tells us that all the futility-causing aspects of life get demolished and consumed. Far from culinary delight, God sets the table to end the nausea of futility.

Futility Swallowed Up

After talking about our change of clothing, Paul reminds us in 2 Corinthians 5:4 that around God's table we will witness "what is mortal" being "swallowed up by life."

Digest the implications:

- Futility eaten for lunch;
- Incompleteness down the gullet;
- Transience chewed up;
- Perishable down the hatch;
- Mortality swallowed up.

1 Corinthians 15:55 uses the same image. Like

2 Corinthians 5:1-4, the dominant imagery of clothing gives way to eating. The perishable will put on a new suit made of the imperishable. The mortal will dress in immortality. Then the image and mood switches.

We move from whispering to shouting. We move from prose to poetry. We move from futility to the Number One Enemy himself.

> Death has been swallowed up in victory.
> Where, O death, is your victory?
> Where, O death, is your sting?
> (1 Corinthians 15:54, 55)

The entree at the final banquet is death. The menace that consumes meek humanity will itself be consumed. The black hood that stalks the race will be destroyed. The haunting fear that has eaten at our souls, taken our loved ones, loomed over our lives will itself be eaten.

Both "swallowing up" texts in the Corinthian letters seem to be dependent on a scene in Isaiah 25. Four chapters (24–27) in the middle of this huge prophetic book peek at the future, some of it the days ahead for Israel, some a look at the end of time. Isaiah paints a picture of a banquet scene, where humanity gathers with God on the top of a mountain. At this banquet, God will deal with the "shroud that enfolds all peoples." Mingling the clothing image with the eating notion reminds us not only of 1 Corinthians 15 and 2 Corinthians 5, but accurately defines that cloak of futility weighing on our lives like a heavy coat bends our shoulders. More complete than the pictures used by Paul, Isaiah gives us an on-the-scene report from that final dinner:

> On this mountain the LORD Almighty will prepare a feast of rich food for all peoples, a banquet

of aged wine. . . . On this mountain he will de-
stroy the shroud that enfolds all peoples, the
sheet that covers over all nations; he will swallow up death forever. The Sovereign LORD will
wipe away the tears from all faces; he will remove the disgrace of his people from all the
earth. The LORD has spoken (Isaiah 25:6-8).

Imagine the scene: The tables bend under the load of
delicacies. The giant banquet hall throngs with
people. Speaking in their native languages, men and
women from every continent, from every ancient
civilization, from every ethnic group mingle around
the mountaintop table. The aroma of the food calls
them to take their seats. The movement of chairs
and the shuffling of feet sound like thunder as the
throng readies for the meal.

All who love God will be there. Take a peek at the
invitation list:

- Our departed parents;
- Dear grandparents;
- Children lost in infancy;
- Teenagers lost in terrible tragedies;
- The lady who invited me to Sunday school;
- The preacher who baptized me into Christ;
- The minister who married Sally and me;
- The people whom God led to him through me;
- Paul, who used Isaiah's imagery about swal-
  lowing up;
- Matthew, Mark, Luke, and John.

As we all sit down to the great feast of the Lamb,
a silence fills the room. We notice that all the chairs
are filled except one. At the head of the giant table,
one chair remains empty. Suddenly the door of the

great banquet hall opens. God appears in the opening. We don't know whether to stand and clap or sit and shout.

We remain silent, struck by the presence of the LORD Almighty. Every set of eyes follows each step as God walks to the table to take his seat. We sit quietly wondering what to do.

Then the door at the other end of the banquet hall opens. A trusted servant enters carrying a large, silver-covered platter. He makes the long walk past the rows of chairs. Eyes from every generation of humanity follow his every step.

Finally, the servant lowers the huge platter in front of God. Every eye in the house stares unblinkingly at the events at the end of the table. Then the servant moves his hand toward the platter. He grasps the handle on the top covering the huge silver plate. Slowly he lifts off the top. Then we see it. Every eye knows immediately what it is. It's the moment we've been waiting for. It marks the end of futility. It means the end of mortality.

There on the platter is the stinking, revolting, ugly mass of death. It's what we've hated all our lives. It represents all the incompleteness, all the tragedy, all the pain, and all the misery of life.

Then God does it. He swallows death. With one great gulp, God ends all the frustration of suffering humanity.

Then God jumps to his feet shouting:

"Victory! VICTORY! *VICTORY!*"

All that's bad, all that's evil, all that's transient, all that's incomplete, all that's futile, all that's threatening, all that's mortal, all that's wrong is swallowed up in victory!

Everything wrong with life, everything we've ever hated, everything that ever weighed on our shoulders is gone. With one swallow, God consumes all that's mortal.

Then God jumps to his feet shouting: "Victory! VICTORY! VICTORY!"

With the wicked out of the way, the giant feast turns festive. Life as we always hoped it would be begins. Joy as we always expected fills our heart. Fulfillment we sought every living day comes to completion in a way beyond what we ever dreamed.

The great banquet breaks forth in praise to God. One group chants, "Glory to God in the highest!"

Another table shouts, "Hallelujah! Hallelujah! Hallelujah!" Praise rises from every tongue. God is glorified in every known language.

Victory has been won!

Fortunately, we get brief glimpses of that banquet and quick samplings of that meal before the day itself. Like Moses in 2 Corinthians 3, God removes the covering on his end-day surprise every once in a while, and we get a glimpse of his glory. Sometimes it comes in prayer. Sometimes in worship. Sometimes in the lives of others.

It was in someone's life that I saw it most clearly.

It was the saddest trip I ever made to the airport. It capped a summer of struggle. Matthew had arrived at the Memphis airport in the late spring. Now in October he was going home. A small army of people gathered to see him off.

One Friday night the previous spring, Matthew had just finished a basketball game with other eleven year olds in his Arkansas hometown when his stomach started to hurt. His mother doctored him from their medicine cabinet. When that didn't work,

they took him to a physician. Soon Matthew was on
a plane to St. Jude's Children's Research Hospital in
Memphis. With a tumor in his body doubling in size
every few hours, the simple stomachache became
life-threatening. The quick trip to Memphis, exami-
nation by top researchers, and immediate treatment
stopped the ugly mass from taking his life.

A day after their arrival in Memphis, a mutual
friend phoned me about their situation. I met Matthew and his parents one rainy May afternoon.
Other Christian friends pulled alongside. Some
loaned cars. Many brought toys or special treats. A
few did laundry. Some just came and talked.

Word from the medical staff went up and down.

"Remission."

"Low blood counts."

"The tumor is growing again."

"Radiation starts Monday."

"Looks good."

"Looks bad."

Finally, in late August, the medical staff gave us
their final word. Not what we hoped for, not what we
wanted. "Take him home. We can do nothing more."

That's why we went to the airport. Our friend
was going home. He died a few weeks later. Over
five hundred people attended his funeral, including
some of his new friends from Memphis. A friend
commented on the large number of children at the
funeral.

The reason Matthew's story is so notable is
because of Matthew. It's not about death. Children
die every day. Yet it became clear in this child's
death that understanding the futility of life, compre-
hending death and dying, depends particularly on
the person who is dying.

In May, when there was just a thread of hope

that the journey to Memphis would not be a death trip, the one who kept up our hopes was Matthew. That's why the little house behind our church building is called the Matthew House. When Old Man Death gazed directly into Matthew's eyes, this boy stared back. He didn't have an indestructible body, but he had a firm belief in forever and a faith in a power named God. Pretty lofty stuff for a preteen.

When the doctors at St. Jude gave up, Matthew kept hoping. As we choked back our tears in the airport terminal, we watched our friend carried off for the final time. Too weak to walk, the lad was carried by his father across the tarmac and up the stairs leading into the Northwest Airlines prop plane. When they reached the top of the stairs, just before they entered the cabin, he did it.

Turning back toward his friends in the terminal, Matthew gave us the "thumbs up" sign.

Matthew probably never read Isaiah 25, but somehow he knew who held the final victory. Despite all the struggles that young man faced and despite all the futility my life still has to offer, I know one thing for certain. Someday, Matthew and I will eat a great banquet together with God.

It was one of those *National Geographic* special reports. Photography superb. Printing excellent. Text clear. Content muddled.

Muddled? The picture abounded in flesh tones, surrounded by dashes of whites, grays, and blacks, but despite the crispness of the reproduction, to me it remained a muddle of flesh tones on a cloudy day. The more I studied the quarter-page photo, the less I understood. Who is this picture about?

Next to the muddled photo, the magazine unfolded

into one of those three-page panorama shots. As I pulled out the folded sheet, the entire creation scene greeted me. It took *National Geographic* three pages to capture the one section from Michelangelo's Sistine Chapel. The bigger picture along with the text told me that the muddled close up of flesh among the drabs was the arm of God separating light from darkness. Once I saw the bigger picture, I understood where the small piece on the previous page fit. The big picture clarified the smaller one.

Nothing illuminates life like the big picture. Nothing brings life into focus like looking at it from eternity. Sitting around God's table relishing victory gives new meaning to releasing our grip. At times it seems that letting go will only lead to disconnected flesh tones amid the dreary colors of a world gone awry. It's only when we see letting go from eternity that we understand that when we release control we drop into the loving arms of God.

Without God's perspective, releasing our grip makes little sense, offers no reward, and seems counterproductive. With God's perspective, it makes no sense at all to hold on. Release the grip. Choose to give him control. Put yourself in his hands.

No matter what happens,
death will be swallowed up by life.

Focusing Your Faith:

1. Reread 2 Corinthians 4:6-9. Define the treasure in this passage.

2. Describe the power Paul is talking about in verse 7.

3. Recall a time when a situation you faced seemed futile; however, in retrospect you realize that God used that situation for a purpose.

4. If you gave God complete control of a current dilemma in your life, how might he be glorified?

5. Hope can be described as "concrete certainty." How certain do you feel about someday coming home to live in the presence of God?

6. At what point in your life did you begin to long for the return of Jesus?

7. What do you look forward to doing first when you join Jesus in glory? Shout for joy? Bow to his feet? Sing his praises? Ask him questions?

EPILOGUE

The Safety Net That Works

I shuddered as I read about the men building Joseph B. Strauss's 4,200-foot span across the entrance to San Francisco Bay. During the five years it took to build the Golden Gate Bridge, the unpredictable gusts of wind surprised one worker after another. Caught off guard, they fell from the bridge hundreds of feet into the ocean below. If the impact with the water didn't kill them, they were pulled under by the current, not to surface again until they reached the Farland Islands.

Fear of falling became a major issue among the workers. High winds canceled work. Caution so immobilized the workers that construction slowed. Holding on with one hand while working with the other offered little progress.

As you might expect from a man who is afraid to clean the second story gutters on his house, working on top of one of Strauss's 476-foot high towers in one of the windiest spots in North America sends me hiding behind the couch. My fear makes me think: forget the bridge, let the people take a ferry. Who needs the world's longest suspension bridge?

That's not what they did back in the 1930s. The workers called a meeting. Fear of falling held up construction. What could they do? How could they proceed? Someone suggested installing a net. Circus performers used a net, why not construction workers? The net was installed. At first the workers didn't trust the swinging rope screen stretched out below, but when the workers who had been swept off the bridge by the latest gust of wind showed up at lunch, not at the morgue, the others became quick believers.

This book has been a meeting of all those who are afraid to let go. We've discussed the net installed below our lives by God himself. Gusty winds will still catch us off guard. We never know where the next windy challenge in life will come from. But underneath all our concerns about finance, friends, family, and future is the swinging rope screen offering security from whatever blows our way.

It's time to let go. That's really the only decision we can make. This book has not offered you steps to find what I found. That's making the mistake of trying to remain in control. What this volume has offered is assurance that God will lead your life if you just loosen your grip.

You are not the first one to face this question. It will not be the last time you make the decision. But for some of us, this meeting of the fearful has taught us that God calls us to take that big step of giving up control. We'll be back to that decision every time the wind starts to gust, every time we crawl out on an unfamiliar cable suspended above the churning ocean below. There will always be new bridges to build, more gutters to clean, more heights to scale.

Our choice is between holding on tight and living in fear, and letting go and living in security. We have to choose which way. We decide whether to release our grip or to squeeze tighter. The only real control we have is to decide to give up control. If we relax our grip, God takes over. He can't release our grip. He won't pry our fingers loose. He won't undo our self-imposed safety belt. But once we unlock the latch, once we open our hand, God's safety net provides all the security we will ever need.

Giving God control opens up a whole new vista on life. The rewards of trusting his net of safety go beyond any meager advantages of working with one hand and holding on with the other. I never expected to find fulfillment in working in the former Soviet Union or in long days of ministry among urban poor or in ten months of writing a book about control. Releasing our grip begins an exciting journey of being surprised by God's wonderful gifts and grace. We'll build bridges we never thought we could build. We'll scale heights we never believed we could climb. We'll sit at banquets we never imagined we'd enjoy.

My journey will not be yours. But God assures us of his guidance. Who knows? Maybe God will bring us together, and I can tell you more about Dan Newton.